One evening when I was rowing the late Admiral Goldsmith (surely one of our most joyful small-boat voyagers) back to his ship in Dartmouth, he suddenly leant towards me and in a stage whisper that must have carried miles:

"I say, old boy," he said, "d'you ever get frightened when you put to sea?"

"Every time, sir," I said.

"So do I, old boy—so do I!"

Peter Pye, The Sea is for Sailing

FOR THE LOVE OF
SAUNTRESS

by
MARTIN O'SCANNALL

with photographs by
OSCAR COMPANIONI

Lodestar Books

Published 2014 by
Lodestar Books
71 Boveney Road, London, SE23 3NL, United Kingdom

www.lodestarbooks.com

A CIP catalogue record for this book
is available from the British Library

ISBN 978-1-907206-26-9

Typeset by Lodestar Books in Equity

Printed in Spain by Graphy Cems, Navarra

All papers used by Lodestar Books
are sourced responsibly

FSC
www.fsc.org
FSC™ C022692

The mark of
responsible forestry

The photographs by Oscar Companioni were taken on a perfect August evening off the Galician coast, during the annual match race between *Sauntress* and her local rival *Abur*.

Contents

to Caroline

1

A Stroke of Luck

"I WONDER IF YOU CAN HELP ME."

"Maybe I could, or maybe I couldn't," was the very Welsh reply. "What is it you are wanting?"

"Would you happen to know of any boats for sale?"

It was a question the young man had asked many times before, and always with the same result. Nothing suited. There was no shortage of boats, but every time there was a problem, either they were too big or too small, or as one honest broker—and yes there is such a thing—remarked, "Don't buy her. She will kill you." It had been a long depressing catalogue of scrabbling about fusty old tore-outs (rotten timber gleaming with suspiciously fresh paint), ugly ducklings, and unspeakable lifeboat conversions. So there was no reason to suppose that this time would be any different.

"What kind of boat is it you are looking for?" with barely concealed cupidity; for an outsider with money to burn in the wilds of the Isle of Anglesey was akin to manna from Heaven.

"Something like that," said the innocent, pointing out a dainty white cutter on her mooring in Holyhead harbour.

"Well," said he "I believe she may just be for sale." He may well have added—but this might just be imagining—"You had better be quick, she is not on the market yet." An Irish horse dealer could not have done it better.

But the laugh is in fact on them. *Sauntress*, for all the paying over the odds, for all the defect in title, and for all her faults, is a little gem from an unknown name, Wright, built by Wright and Harris in Cardiff, Wales, in 1913, barely a year before the outbreak of the Great War. In short a product of the Indian summer of the great age of yacht building, when the finest materials went into the humblest of vessels and labour was cheap.

She measures 28ft overall, excluding bowsprit, 22ft on the waterline, 8ft beam, 4ft 10in draught, is built of pitch pine on steamed oak frames and is a classic gaff cutter of her time. Of her history before my ownership I know nothing more than can be gleaned from her Certificate of British Registry, which is a mere succession of names and addresses going back to 1948, but which showed her to have been based on the East Coast of England, and to have changed hands annually.

This last, perhaps, should have been a warning that all was not well, but in the first flush of ownership one tends to gloss over the unpalatable: her funny little habit of missing stays; the Stuart Turner petrol engine which could seldom be coaxed into life; her lovely sheer marred by hogging; and the interminable drive every weekend, just to be with her.

Summer melted imperceptibly into autumn.

She was careened, delightful word, for no better reason than I wanted to, and perhaps to give her a scrub. Line run ashore from the masthead, anchor laid out to seaward, she lay at an angle on the beach, my pride and joy. All this was of course just playing, rowing off at midnight, pausing under the moon to admire her shapely counter, lighting the oil lamps, a little excursion round the harbour, picking up the mooring under sail, a romantic bubble which sooner or later would have to be pricked; for Holyhead, as a base for *Sauntress*, was impractical and it was high time to go.

2

On the Wings of Chance

THERE IS, REMARKS MAURICE GRIFFITHS somewhere in his writings, a little cherub that looks after inexperienced sailors; until, that is, she tires and moves on elsewhere.

In the background lurked a guru, an eccentric, locked away in a house of indescribable disorder, who in the way of such gurus had a powerful hold on a young imagination. And this guru, Alan was his name, saw nothing remotely unwise in dispatching his young protégé down the Irish Sea, across the entrance to the Bristol Channel and as far up channel as may be, at a time when all self-respecting craft should be abed for the winter.

So when Alan sniffed the air and announced it was time to go, I needed no second bidding. Provided with a crew, one Gordon, whose chief if not only claim to fame was an ability to dismantle Land Rovers allied with, as it transpired, an entirely spurious air of manliness, a borrowed radio direction finder and some rather moth-eaten charts, away *Sauntress* went.

Smiting Holyhead breakwater with that shapely counter by way of adieu, for she missed stays again, we were soon off South Stack running before a brisk north-easter, Gordon ashen grey leaning over the cockpit coaming, violently seasick.

The guardian angel might be forgiven for raising a sceptical eyebrow. But the sea glittered, *Sauntress* raced southwards, dipping the main (*peak it up Martin, peak it up,* but I did not then know that kind of thing), we reeled off the miles in exhilarating fashion, for this was *Sauntress* on her very first passage in my ownership, than which there is no greater thrill. The log reflects this mixture of pride, not to say hubris:

"Still running like mad; quite steep seas but regular and steady wind, white horses but not threatening; *Sauntress* really swooping along, Log 39."

Over the bow in an otherwise empty sea, although quite where we were was another matter, appeared a French fishing boat which turned and hailed us "Force 10," an incident logged rather fatuously as "forecast 7 so not too worried" with the heartless addition "crew still unwell."

We ploughed on regardless, the tiring business of steering a gaff cutter on a dead run being shared watch on watch. The radio direction finder slumbered, neglected; below, the log spun merrily, the course was steered, more or less, and night fell.

It was time for the navigation lights.

These, like all else on *Sauntress*, were of an ancient and handsome design, all brass and fuelled by paraffin. Filling them on a heaving cabin sole was both nauseating and pointless, for no sooner than installed, they blew out. We sailed on, a darkened ship.

The southern entrance to the Irish Sea is marked by two powerful lights, Tuskar on the Irish side and The Smalls on the Welsh side. We saw neither, though we did see shore lights to starboard, which should have alerted us to the fact that we were rather to the west of our intended course.

In striking distance of the equinox (it was early October) the nights were long and cold. The yacht yawed rather, for we were still running before Alan's promised northerly, and tiredness began to extend its stealthy tentacles.

But dawn, still bright, brought renewed vigour, and a second day running before the wind, still watch on watch. Already the log entries have dwindled to a trickle, "0830 log 126" is followed by "2200. Hand over to Gordon saying I hope to raise the Scillies in the night." Still the radio direction finder slumbered below. In a slightly more seamanlike world, we could have hove to, gathered our wits a little, figured things out, taken a fix and made a new departure. But no, we ploughed on.

"0200. On watch again, no sign of Scillies by dawn, as expected" which, in the circumstances is not to be wondered at. Indeed the wonder is that we had not piled up somewhere. But the guardian angel, tugging maybe at the tiller, had dumped us unceremoniously in the western approaches, as we discovered when it occurred to us to press the radio direction finder into service; 40 miles west of Round Island, to be exact. The time was 0900 on day three.

Gordon chose this moment to set course for America. Which little contretemps remedied, we raised Bishop Rock, log 315, at 2000 on the same day. Watch on watch as ever.

"Aim" said I, most unwisely, "for that light" and turned in. Never, but never, tell your crew—never mind an inexperienced crew—to "aim for that light." For Gordon did just that. Wolf Rock, for it was Wolf Rock at which I had instructed Gordon to aim, must be very steep to, for I was awoken by the remarkable sight of the thing looming overhead. We scuttled clear.

Autumn, in the shape of a depression, made itself felt, and as day four dawned it was to a grey and restless sea, a rising wind and deteriorating visibility. "Seas bad enough to have to steer looking at waves coming up astern," reads the log bleakly. "Gordon gybes the boat. Jib tears. Decide for Falmouth. *Sauntress* will not make up against 'full gale' so heavily reefed set course for Prawle Point."

Oh dear, how many dramas in those few words.

The shock of the gybe. *Sauntress* out of control. The broach. The jib flogging for a moment before disintegrating. The struggle on the foredeck. And the awful realisation that there, all too clearly, is *Sauntress*' Achilles' heel. For nothing on earth would induce her to go to windward.

Thoroughly dispirited we ran off, as the log says, for Prawle Point.

Never mind that there were several perfectly good harbours between Falmouth and Prawle Point. For some reason a fixation had crept in and that fixation was Dartmouth. The log entries petered out. This complete disintegration of rational thought processes has been chronicled many times. The simplest task becomes impossibly difficult. Reasoning is replaced by wishful thinking. Obsessions take hold. You become desperate for the endless motion, the endless noise, and the endless discomfort, to stop.

The murk closed in and when it cleared a headland appeared. "That, Gordon is Prawle Point." A piece of wishful thinking which had us entering Mevagissey under the impression it was Dartmouth.

How did we know?

The Mevagissey Arms read a sign on a pub.

We sailed out again into the gathering dusk. Why? I cannot answer that. But we did. Gordon understandably mutinied, taking no further interest in proceedings.

Dartmouth. It had to be Dartmouth.

Sauntress, like a moth to a flame now, had Eddystone in her sights. The topping lift tangled with the cross-trees. The skipper, torch in mouth, spent an interminable time bouncing on the foredeck, obsessively clearing the tangle, Eddystone winking all the while. Why in the hell can't we get clear of this **** light?

But at last we did.

I handed back to the reluctant mutineer, who found the race off Start Point and spent the night gybing the boat, skipper too tired to care.

Dawn came at last. We shook out the reefs and shaped up for Dartmouth; the object of my obsession, Dartmouth.

The tide was running off.

The Stuart Turner would run but had no power.

A tow was offered and accepted.

And the guardian angel folded her arms with an only-too-audible sigh.

The year was 1973. *Sauntress* was 60. Her owner was 28. It would be twelve years before her keel touched the water again.

3

Handy with a Toolbox

A LOVELY IRISH EXPRESSION THAT ONE, in full "seven brothers and all handy with a toolbox," quoted in Sneem, Kenmare River, County Kerry; but we were not there yet, not by a long chalk.

Instead we were in the seedy purlieus of West London, Brentford Dock to be exact, one of those havens which had escaped the developers. For behind a high wall lay John Woolley's little empire, a boatyard, the boats in question being narrow-boats with their floating gypsy-caravan livery, and beyond that the greenery of Syon Park, from which the screech of an invisible peacock could occasionally be heard.

And the lap and gurgle of the Grand Union Canal or, more like, the occasional burp, as something nasty rose from the depths. For only by the wildest stretch of the imagination could this be called a marine environment; but at least there was water.

And here, very much in bits, was *Sauntress*, victim of a particularly bad attack of gleeful destruction, a bare hull open to the skies, her owner slightly aghast at the enormity of the deed.

But the destruction, though brutal, was necessary.

A hogged sheer is no thing of beauty so the first job was to remedy that. A bare hull, as *Sauntress* now was, is a relatively flimsy thing. A jack, or more correctly in this case an Acrow prop, exerts enormous power, quite enough to force the topsides back to something approaching their original position. The rest can be, and in this case was, done by planing back the irregularities in the sheer. Now *Sauntress* once again had a sheer sweet to the eye.

To keep it that way, six pairs of sawn oak frames supplemented her obviously inadequate steamed timbers. Working oak with a pruning saw, fitting, refitting and refitting again until the bevel was perfect, was not a quick job but it would not be done again, so it had to be right. And manifestly was right, for they have never moved since.

The next step was to attack the tenderness. Here the keel, which was iron, was dropped six inches and the gap filled with concrete. This slightly eyebrow-raising approach looks less outlandish when one considers that concrete was even, if not especially, used internally in quality work, witness Claud Worth's *Tern III*. In any event it stiffened the boat up and so, in a subsequent refit and a moment of relative prosperity, the old iron keel was removed, recast in lead and refitted minus the concrete.

That done, the more pleasant task of recreating *Sauntress* as I wanted her to be in my mind's eye could begin. For this was no faithful restoration of the original, except Wright's lovely hull. Instead what kind of cabin, what kind of interior layout, what sort of deck, what kind of cockpit, were simply a matter of what would work best, be strongest, and look the part. And look the part meant be in keeping with a yacht of *Sauntress'* age and period.

Strength came from new oak carlins, tie-bolted to the beam shelf, massive lodging knees bolted to the main beam and carlins forward, and two new oak beams at deck level aft, where the cabin was to divide from the cockpit.

More strength came from what might be called a composite construction: steel in a wooden ship in the shape of a long steel girder across the floors, longitudinally, with web frames welded on and bolted to the new oak frames, the whole treated against corrosion.

Before a deck could be laid a decision had to be made on what kind of cabin. Not too high, for the quest for standing headroom had produced the ugly doghouse, now consigned to the rubbish. Nor necessarily did it have to be the conventional rectangular box. So the decision was made that the forward end should be rounded, New Zealand yacht style (of the period) on the basis that it was pretty, and more spuriously that it offered less resistance to a wave breaking aboard.

That was built, in teak. The decision to use teak was simply that it was the best timber available, and by best is meant the most durable, pleasant to work and pleasant to the eye.

The deck was more problematic. Almost all restorations or rebuilds use a plywood sub-deck, but I dislike ply and questioned the rigidity of the material in a wooden hull, which by its nature flexes a little in a seaway. So instead Columbian pine, which is extremely light, was laid as a sub-deck. This was fastened with silicon bronze grip-fast nails, and splined. A liquid rubber compound was painted over and a teak deck laid over that, screwed down with marine grade stainless steel screws, plugged.

The scantlings of the teak were such that it could wear over the years without distortion. This deck was not swept as, say, in a Fife boat, but laid straight, which I prefer. It gives a touch of the workman-like or sinewy strength which is the hallmark of *Sauntress*. It has lasted some 40 years and looks as handsome as ever.

The first cockpit was less of a success as, amongst other things, a large and heavy Coventry Victor single cylinder diesel engine had to be accommodated under the bridge deck; but when that, and its successor—a Japanese engine—were removed and auxiliary power dispensed with, a teak, once again self-draining, cockpit was installed, with a small well which ensured that if a green sea did come aboard, as happened once, the water could drain safely away. Teak washboards replaced cabin doors.

The boat is sailed single-handed or two-handed, so when it came to fitting out the interior she would need to sleep two, or very occasionally three. She was to have a good galley, and a separate chart table and seat for chart work, and once again she had to look of the period, something of the Edwardian yacht. (That incidentally was one reason for preferring the splined sub deck, no expanses of white painted plywood to stare at from one's bunk, but instead a proper deckhead.)

She also had to accommodate a six-foot crew in comfort when he or she was sleeping below. That meant a settee berth in the main cabin of six feet six inches. For this and quite a few other details I had Donald Street's

The Ocean Sailing Yacht to thank. For I had plans for little *Sauntress* when I was done.

Thus, the layout as you enter the cabin is as follows. To port is the chart table and navigator's seat. All internal joinery, unless otherwise specified, is varnished mahogany, in places inlaid with ebony, an expensive and strange wood, but undeniably handsome. Next came the 6ft 6in berth, extending when needed to a double, ending conveniently under the main beam, and separated from the forward part of the vessel by a tongue-and-groove cream painted pine bulkhead. Above is a fiddled shelf for such things as the Walker log, binoculars and GPS, and under the navigator's seat lives the sextant.

Opposite the navigator, with small folding seat set into the teak steps, is the galley: double sink, Taylor's stainless steel oven, general galley stowage. Beyond that, and departing from the norm, is a settee, with octagonal swing table, beyond which a sideboard, and facing the main bunk a charcoal stove. Glasses (whisky) and bottles stow behind the settee, and the sideboard houses the barograph and main cabin oil lamp. This has the inestimable twin advantages that it can be turned low, for sailing at night, and to keep the chill off the air at anchor. Electricity is kept to the minimum, powered by solar panel and used for the chart table, galley, navigation lights and compass light.

This arrangement means that the navigator does not disturb the sleeping crew, and the cook disturbs neither.

Forward and to starboard is what has become the owner's bunk, private and undisturbed there, with the hanging locker and heads opposite, and right up forward, stowage for sails.

This, approximately—for some of the changes came later—was the layout and structure of the yacht as she emerged from John Woolley's yard after twelve years. And in this form she has been sailing ever since (save the discarding of the engine which will be discussed later).

Her rig is the classic gaff cutter arrangement, with topsail and increasing large sail wardrobe, with Wykeham-Martin furling gear on jib and foresail, and peak and throat halyards led back to the cockpit for ease of handling when single-handing. She now also carries a square sail and yard, the latter permanently aloft and the former sent up on three halyards. Claud Worth describes this arrangement in detail in *Yacht Navigation and Voyaging*.

We were ready to go back to sea.

4

A Kind of Swallows and Amazons

"AT SCARCELY MORE THAN A DRIFT, ghoster barely filling, the old girl stemmed the spring ebb. Slowly Spaniard, swinging rhythmically in the tide, slipped astern. It was going to take several hours yet to reach the anchorage in the Swale, but we were in no hurry, it was a perfect summer's evening, and the holiday was almost over.

No time to be starting engines.

Night was falling as the chain rattled out, and in the stillness that followed only the familiar call of the birds broke the silence. Low tide, flat calm, complete solitude, mud flats all around, a warm cabin lit by oil lamps, the day's charts tidied away, and supper on the stove beckoned a tired skipper.

But for the moment, sitting quietly in the cockpit, as dusk drew in and the lights of Whitstable began to wink in the distance, and reflecting on the excitements of the long summer's cruise, there was no doubt where the old hooker was most at home; it was here amongst the creeks and inlets of the East Coast."

* * *

"A day made perfect by its enchanting finish, patient beat to the Swin, close reach at some speed down the Whittaker channel, then in failing wind, gentle and ever gentler tack up the Roach, setting sun, birds and with barely more than steerage way, creep along the edge of the slowly covering mud, to anchor in solitude in Yoke Creek.

Three quarter moon. And a cow on the saltings, peering at this lone apparition."

*   *   *

No, this is not Maurice Griffiths, but *Sauntress'* log, random extracts amongst many because, like the great man, *Sauntress* was utterly seduced by the east coast rivers, where after the long refit she was based. And where, drawing a discreet veil over a certain incident in the oddly-named Leigh Ray Gut, to do with an onshore force seven and another bit of bungling, *Sauntress* had settled down to become just another gaff cutter, pottering, cruising or racing as the mood took.

The world had changed whilst *Sauntress* had been in hibernation. No longer would we hear the comment "would convert nicely to Bermudan." For the revival of interest in gaff rig was in full swing, and if not in the mood for creeping to the head of some creek in splendid isolation there was racing, there were rallies, indeed all the fun of the fair.

And there was Crispin.

Who leapt aboard on a very windy day on the River Deben to become the first of a series of faithful crew. It was not my fault that we almost immediately ran aground, and spent the rest of what had until that point been an exciting race through the moorings at Waldringfield, sitting at an angle on a shingle bank. But running aground in the rivers was par for the course and perfectly safe, if a little public.

Out in the estuary it would be a very different matter, for there you would like or not lose your ship. And that, the contrast, is part of the appeal. One moment you are thrashing up the Wallet, or dodging, heart in mouth, in poor visibility through those lethal sands, and the next, drifting, mainsheet kissing the water, to some anchorage.

But Crispin, as well as being crew, also had his own yacht, almost the same size and vintage as *Sauntress*, and from there it was but a small step to the inevitable challenge. His partner Edith was called Webb, his yacht *Wendy*, from which, for we were playing how to enjoy yourself on the East Coast, came the deathless, every bit as exciting as the America's Cup and a damn sight cheaper:

Webb's Wonder Challenge Trophy 1990
for the title
The Most Bloody-Minded Skipper

Wendy had to her credit two firsts (Stour Passage Race and Maldon Anniversary Rally) and one third (Ipswich Race).

Sauntress had two firsts (Deben Passage Race, Swale First Visiting Yacht) one second (Maldon Anniversary) and one third (Swale Match).

Sauntress had just pipped *Wendy* in the OGA Race—but one of her firsts (Visiting Yacht) was a bit spurious. Equally, *Sauntress* felt *Wendy*'s first in the anniversary rally would have been more convincing had *Wendy* single-handed.

Sauntress however had forfeited her "Most Bloody-Minded Skipper" prize by weakly retiring, when leading *Wendy*, in the Stour Rally race, which *Wendy* deservedly won.

Day 1

Dawned with atrocious visibility, no wind and a forecast "perhaps 8."

Sauntress made her way to the start, Bateman's Wreck—in no visibility, and by echo sounder and compass—and waited for *Wendy* to appear. *Wendy* anchored opposite, invisibly and waited for *Sauntress* to appear.

At 1125 the mist cleared and an 1135 start was agreed. *Sauntress* fouled her anchor and, by the time she was under way, was late and badly positioned downwind of *Wendy* to clear Mersea point close hauled against a SE zephyr.

Sauntress however found a useful back-eddy to cheat the flood tide, and hugging the shore made up ground as *Wendy* stemmed the tide.

One up for tactics to *Sauntress*.

But *Wendy* held and extended her lead over *Sauntress* in the drift down to the edge of Mersea flats, *Sauntress* trying her spinnaker (aback!) in the fluky and frustrating airs and then crossing to the eastern side of the channel in search of wind.

Wendy lost to view but ahead when last seen.

Wendy apparently anchored. *Sauntress* found another strong back-eddy or early ebb, and wind as well, and quickly made up along the St Osyth shore in four feet, till almost abreast of the Inner Bench Head, wind now SW instead of SE. Her tack across to Inner Bench Head lost her the tide and most of the wind, but she managed to round the mark ahead.

Luck, or tactics, to *Sauntress* again.

Visibility much better, but still poor. *Sauntress* whipped up her spinnaker, but *Wendy* quickly set her light-airs jib, and ate up *Sauntress'* lead. *Sauntress*, getting a bit desperate, tried another tactical board into the St Osyth shore and then across to Mersea Flats as *Wendy* majestically forged ahead. Suddenly fog—with a vengeance—so *Sauntress*, again in shallow water, again steered by compass, sound (from the land) and sounder N by E hoping for luck.

It came.

The fog rolled away and a nice little easterly found *Sauntress* hurrying back across from the St Osyth shore in pursuit of a relatively becalmed, mist- and tide-bound *Wendy*. By Bateman's Wreck *Sauntress* had recouped all but a boat length of the lead before the breeze failed, fog rolled back from the west and efforts to fight it out up Pyefleet were frustrated, both yachts drifting backwards.

Day abandoned—result inconclusive.

Day 2

Forecast F5–7 increasing 8 and this time it was obviously going to blow. Three reefs and foresail only for *Sauntress*, many rolls and small foresail for *Wendy*. Shortened course agreed, Inner Bench Head, up to Alresford and down again.

All secure below, rather nervous (on *Sauntress* anyway) in a definitely F6 and strengthening, there proved to be a good deal of S in the forecast easterly. This time it was *Sauntress* who made the better start, though arguably early across the line, but with *Wendy* snapping at her heels.

Sauntress was having difficulty seeing, and with glasses on was troubled with spray, glasses off blind, so concerned not to be driven down on Mersea flats in these strong winds; made up easterly, *Wendy* doggedly following, and the seas building as Colne Bar and the open water neared.

Wendy saw the mark before *Sauntress* and disappeared downwind, but when *Sauntress* finally spotted the mark, her eased sheets and her ability to drive over the waves started to count, giving her perhaps 100 yards as she rounded Inner Bench Head, getting well clear of the buoy before choosing her moment to tack; even so she hung in stays with foresail backed for quite a while before bearing away, with undisguised relief, for calmer waters and friendly mud.

The broad reach suited *Sauntress*, and *Wendy*, having missed stays, had little to give in answer as both yachts re-entered the Colne, *Sauntress* perhaps five minutes ahead. Both set their jibs, *Sauntress* to maintain her lead, *Wendy* to close, and *Wendy* was making up bit by bit as *Sauntress* gybed round the Alresford mark for the last leg home; very close hauled, this last stretch, strong gusts, but relative calm in between, and *Sauntress*' old inability to make to windward as well as she should began to tell, laid over in the gusts, pinching as far as she dared, for she could not keep *Wendy* off for long, but just, only just, squeezed by Bateman's Wreck Buoy, perhaps 50 yards ahead.

A winner?

Technically yes, but the bloody-minded skipper prize must be shared for racing, single handed, in a gale.

Such are the joys of East Coast sailing.

5

Mud, Mud, Glorious Mud

THERE IS, IN JACK COOTE'S 1957 EDITION of *East Coast Rivers*, a delightful photograph of his 11-ton centreboarder *Iwunda* at rest on the sedge grass of Horsey Mere, with the sounding pole, marked black and white in feet, stowed up and down the port shroud. And that should tell you we are very close to Arthur Ransome's *Secret Water*, the Walton Backwaters.

Chris and I on a cold but bright March day had set off from our mooring on the Orwell for a typical East Coast cruise, out through Harwich Harbour, pick up the Pye End buoy (always difficult to spot) and thence up the Walton Channel for the obligatory beer; for Chris, fine shipmate that he was, would interrupt what was otherwise a gentle drift, communing with nature, with

"What about a pint?"

So pint it had to be.

Now whether that had something to do with it, or the skipper was being a little careless, or, as the log records, trying for a good angle on the withy at the narrow part of the channel, we touched, just at the point where Hamford Water joins the Walton Channel, and it being a spring ebb, once you are on the mud, you are on.

There was no point in recriminations. The thing was done, so we launched the dinghy, laid out the kedge and as the tide receded were surprised to find that *Sauntress* simply settled, completely upright, in a thank-you-very-much-this-suits-me sort of way, into the mud.

So there for the time being we left her, looking very picturesque, whilst we walked on the beach at Stone Point. Later in the season and at a weekend, this popular anchorage would be packed with boats, but on a weekday and in

March we had the place to ourselves. Harwich and Felixstowe would soon be twinkling distantly, but here nothing but the breeze, the whispering in the grass, the popping of the mud as the tide ran off, and of course the birds. Until, from Chris

"What have we got for supper?"

The man had no soul, first a pint, now food. But he had a point so as we boarded *Sauntress* once again it was with a bucket of mussels picked at low tide.

Now came a tiny breeze from the west, just as the sun dipped behind Hamford Water, and as *Sauntress* stirred and then gently broke free on a rising tide, we slipped across to Stone Point to anchor and feast on freshly harvested mussels.

It rained and blew in the night but here we were perfectly safe, and the forecast in the morning being SW 4 to 5 occasionally 6, we tucked in a couple of reefs; Chris broke out the anchor and we were away, with more north in the wind than expected, pinching and lee-bowing down to Pye End, a smart beat up the Stour, still no other boats around, sneak a look at Gas House Creek, alarmingly shallow, run off back down again, across Shotley Spit inside the barges, and now against a spring ebb, tack on tack, skies clear, to our mooring.

"Jolly good exercise and jolly good fun," reads the log.

Which is no more than the truth.

6

Going Foreign

I FORGET WHOSE IDEA IT WAS, but for some reason an idea had formed, and once formed, worried like some irritating fly until there was nothing for it: *Sauntress* would have to venture to Holland. Quite why we should wish to exchange the simple pleasures of the Essex rivers for the chimera that is 'going foreign' beats me, but there it was. Nor did I view the prospect with unalloyed pleasure, for though not a long passage in terms of distance it was fraught with unpleasant possibilities.

There would be shipping to contend with. The shoals and banks on the other side needed treating with respect. And as a glance at the tidal atlas shows, the tides run hard, in places very hard. Not only that, but unlike the East Coast there were no friendly rivers in which to anchor for the night, only a nasty lee shore and harbours and docks of somewhat evil reputation; in short, not a passage to be undertaken lightly.

The skipper, chastened by what was forever after known as 'The Mevagissey Incident,' was somewhat better prepared, having worked his way through the entire RYA syllabus to emerge theoretically equipped for Astro Navigation and the avoidance of Tropical Revolving Storms (unlikely in the North Sea) but more importantly with a reasonably firm grip on the fundamentals of pilotage in the pre-GPS era.

For in that pre-electronic age you found your way about by distance run, the faithful Walker towed log, compass course (corrected for deviation, variation and leeway) and a little game called tidal triangles, that insidious force which carries your vessel if you pay no attention, way off course. All this backed up by fixing your position at every opportunity.

But there is more. As our planning showed us, the tides in the Wester-schelde, at the head of which lay Vlissingen, our proposed landfall, run very hard, a phenomenon already familiar to any East Coast yachtsman, hence the refrain "work your tides." For three knots against you, when you sail at five, means two knots over the ground. Whilst three knots with you, when you sail at five, means eight knots over the ground. This arithmetic apart, the upshot is that either you whizz along or stand still.

Thus we timed our passage to arrive at West Hinder light vessel at low water, in the expectation of being squirted up the Westerschelde like the pro-verbial dose of salts.

But the best laid plans of mice and men…

Chris "time for a pint" Race was crew. And as solid a crew as you could wish for. Skipper of his own vessel, meticulous to a fault, strong, reliable, un-flappable, but you had to be sure there was a pub somewhere.

The log of that trip, and all others, I still have. It shows that at 0730 on 20 July we left Kirby Creek motoring, these were the Coventry Victor, wildly-eccentric-but-it-works-kind-of, days, butting into an ENE 4-5, cleared Pye End at 0840, set the main with two reefs plus foresail and laid off courses to clear, respectively (all dutifully logged as to their bearing, time of sighting, distance run), Medusa, NE Gunfleet, Trinity, Long Sand Head, Galloper; crossed, at the mandatory right angle, the Traffic Separation Scheme; crossed two arms of Fairy Bank (we knew that by echo sounder) and raised, fine on the port bow, West Hinder, our nautical signpost at 1800, which was low water; so far, precisely as planned.

Bringing the laconic entry, "DR fine."

Then however came a douche of cold water in the shape of the 1755 ship-ping forecast which was logged as "NE backing N" (good) "increasing 6 to 7" (ouch!) "squally showers."

But we hardly needed to be told, for within the hour came the entry:

"1920 NE by E 3, visibility good, course 93° log 63 ¼ mile south Oost Dyk nasty sky"

And hard on the heels of that:

"1947 N by E 5, Visibility good, course 93°, log 65 now full fair tide up Westerschelde, triple reef, furl jib only by running off to reduce windage. Wind N by E 6 and rising."

And here, for all our planning, lay the fly in the ointment. For whilst our full fair tide, all six hours of it, would undoubtedly send us whizzing up the Westerschelde, it would be in the teeth of a F7 squally wind, definition of a squall, by the way, being a sustained increase in the wind force, of in this case one Beaufort notation, for at least one minute. In short, force 7 with gusts of F8, which is, thank you very much, gale force.

Thus we were about to make the acquaintance of another well-known phenomenon, wind over tide, indeed a strong wind over a strong tide, with the delightful added ingredients of a pitch dark night, dangerous shoals if we should but stray, and a positive procession of merchant vessels in, quote "one of the busiest shipping lanes in the world" unquote.

Lovely.

We then discovered we had knocked the Heath Robinson ignition switch off and in some way flattened the battery, so no navigation lights.

"2015. N by E 6 and rising, twilight, log 67, ¼ mile S Azuid. Hand start engine to charge, Chris off watch"

And, now alone on watch,

"2056 N by E 6 – 7 log 71 Kwintebank, dark."

Surprisingly, there were log entries to record what had suddenly become quite an exciting night. For what lay ahead if we did not pile up and nothing broke was a 50 mile stretch very close on the wind, up the Westerschelde. As the log records there were moments of confusion and the odd scare.

"2056 to 2230 N b E 7, buoy hopping. Made up to windward, mistake, in channel and ships in all directions, scuttle clear, waves hiding lights, making identification difficult," reads one entry.

"2230 N by E 7, at Group cardinals, muddled, call Chris, run off then tack west then south of danger, dodge ship" reads the next.

"2245 N by E 7, buoy hopping all the way, wave taken green squirts water through coachroof ventilator, very wet below, pump often."

"2400 approximately, clear Zeebrugge, seas less, wind still very strong, still buoy hopping, shore lights all too close under our lee."

And so on...

But, here in all the noise, motion and general misery of this perfectly horrible passage, engraved as it is in my memory, one thing was being proved beyond doubt. *Sauntress* was up to it. She might be lurching and crashing, taking waves green, down below a kind of demented washing machine, but praise be, she was making up to windward, standing up to her canvas and, mile by painful mile, gaining the shelter of the land.

And that, in the end, that was all that mattered.

There is little to add. I managed to try to ram a ship, confused by the bridge lights; dawn came, or at least an apology for dawn, the waves eased as the tide turned, and the delights of the commercial harbour we call Flushing (curiously apt given the state of the harbours on this coast) beckoned.

There is a small postscript.

It is easy to exaggerate the wind force, perhaps especially at night. So we checked with both the UK and Dutch Meteorological Offices (I would not bother now, but then we were as keen as mustard.) And yes, little *Sauntress* had fought her way 50 miles to windward in a F7 wind gusting 8 and waves of 2.5 metres. Or so they say.

I find the F8 hard to believe.

The next little itch would take us further, but that is another story.

7

Orford

Directions for entry 1986:

From a position about two cables North East of the Red and White Buoy moored four and a half cables 144° True from the Coast Guard Cottages (52.02.01 N 1.27.4 E) proceed, keeping Hollesey Church Tower, situate eleven cables North West of the Coastguard Cottages, bearing about 308° True and midway between the Coastguard Cottages and Bungalow, 1 cable North East.

When the beacon, Orange diamond top mark, situate 5 cables North East of the Coastguard Cottages comes into line with prominent chimney (One mile North East of the beacon), bearing 002° True, follow this leading mark which passes west of the new shingle islet (dries 2 metres) lying two cables East South East of the bungalow.

When abreast the ruined ramp, two cables south of beacon, alter North East to pass close to West of North West Point.

Keep close to the East side of the river so as to avoid the shoal tongue, which extends into the middle of the river from the West side.

When past the beacon continue midstream.

NOT ALL, YOU SEE, IS FRIENDLY MUD, for once north of Harwich things begin to change. Bleak, bleak and threatening, are the shingle banks which now stretch unbroken up this coast, and if the Deben bar is tricky, the Ore is more so. And yet this is one of the most haunting and beautiful of all the rivers, for once in, the river winds, in utter tranquillity, for miles up, should you ever reach it, to Snape Maltings, the haunt of Thames barges, Benjamin Britten and a certain amount of flummery. But you do not have to go there.

And I, for one, never have, for the withies are few, the broad stretch of water at high tide conceals a narrow winding channel, with not a buoy in sight, so most probably you will stick, as we stuck, in glutinous mud.

But the bar is a different proposition. Ever-changing, with each season if not each storm, it is a thing to be respected. In a south-easterly gale the place is a maelstrom, not even to be attempted. The old way in was by semaphore, the coastguard on the beach flagging your vessel this way or that, trust him, you must trust him, however close those shingle banks; but now, or at least then, for we are many years back, this little chartlet was your guide, that and your nerve.

But, as a little challenge, changing pastime to sport, the place was irresistible, for once in, the sea could roar on the shingle outside, the clouds could scurry across the sky, wind bending the reeds, but your vessel, at anchor in the Butley river, would be as safe as safe could be.

And there was always the spice of getting out again.

Which is why, almost every season, it was one little passage that had to be made, armed with your 25p chartlet and, as the sailing directions will tell you, a good powerful engine, for getting out on the flood; you must stem a five-knot tide, be ready for the eddies, and above all keep your nerve.

And should you not have an engine?

The barges of old did it and one at least still does. Her name is *Edme*. And *Edme* takes us to the head of another creek, just one out of so many and *Edme* plays, as we later learned to play, at doing it the old way, the entrance to the Ore and all. *Edme*—English Diastatic Malt Extract—is an 80ft Thames sailing barge and her home, in winter anyway, is at St Osyth, known to all as Toosey. And her owners, the Harman family.

Funny place, Essex.

Just down the road are the delights of Clacton. Essex girl was a byword for 1980s brashness. But here was another Essex, the old Essex, the Essex of the smacksmen, the bargemen, the bawleys, of James Lawrence, of The Company Shed, of that slow burr, of large timbers, of Stockholm tar, of cordage, of some strange mix, the name of which I forget, but which dyed her several tons of mainsail—and all who came into contact with it—the obligatory ochre, a glorious and surely poisonous witches brew.

And *Edme*, I remember, doing it the old way, decided the nice clean shingle piled up on the bar at the entrance to the Ore, that place of five-knot tides, was just the thing for ballast. On the excellent premise that if their forerunners could do it, why not they.

So it is not in fact playing. It is more. A kind of paying respects to ancestors. Or perhaps a bit of both. And a test of seamanship.

And all the while a little seed was germinating…

But not yet.

8

Toosey

and a lesson learned

L
IKE ALL THE BEST PLACES, St Osyth boatyard is a little scruffy. The
kind of place which makes officialdom nervous. In the mud berths lie a
collection of more-or-less derelict vessels, some liveaboards, some hopeless
dreams, and others merely awaiting the spring refit. And there, swan amongst
ducklings, is *Edme*, her great topmast soaring.

And just down a little unmade road, before the row of flint cottages with
their gardens running down to the creek, are a slipway, a trolley, a large winch
and a couple of corrugated iron sheds.

And more likely than not, a smack up on the hard, awaiting attention.
Investigate the shed and you might find Alan Williams, shipwrighting or
having a cup of tea, or Andy Harman, about to move something impossibly
heavy, or Droid completing his thirty-odd-foot, one-day-I-will-sail-to-the-
Azores, wooden yacht.

It was, in short, the perfect place for *Sauntress,* and having found it I never
once thought of going anywhere else. For here you could work peacefully and
companionably. No-one interfered. You were given a key and came and went
as you like. It is the antithesis of a marina, is untidy, but is warm and comfortable like an old and much-loved coat.

And for me, at least, Toosey meant all the pleasures of the spring refit,
that wonderful feeling of anticipation of the coming season. They were long
hours of work, up with the proverbial lark and to bed with the sun, but I never begrudged them. Here I fashioned *Sauntress'* lovely octagonal mahogany
table. Here I made the curved back for the chart table seat. Here I remade
the hatch garage and here, later, I put in the teak self-draining cockpit. To

the accompaniment I think of mildly amused curiosity as yet another piece of expensive tropical hardwood succumbed to the saw.

But if you love your boat, and I certainly love *Sauntress*, you give her your best, whatever that may be. And then comes that moment when at last you stop sawing, hoover out the shavings and start on the paint and the varnish. And watch, in something approaching wonderment, as wood, that living thing, which makes another living thing, a sailing boat, leaps to life.

That final touch before the season starts.

And for those who say that varnish is too much trouble, or that paint is too much trouble, or that wooden boats are too much trouble, well each to his own. But you cannot help wondering just what else might be too much trouble, the things which not only beautify your boat but on which her safety relies.

And the proof of this attitude, which goes far beyond mere appearance, but is rooted in that, is that virtually every one of the smacks and barges, the aristocrats of the East Coast, which certainly require a great deal of work, are not only beautifully maintained, but beautifully sailed too.

No wonder, perhaps, that at times they look slightly down their noses at the rest of us.

But you have, ahem, having applied the last lick of varnish, cleaned your brushes and tidied all away, to get out of the impossible ditch that is Toosey creek, at the top of the tide; for if not there is no water and this, as the denizens of the yard know all too well, is the moment for some good clean fun.

For the ditch, sorry creek, is unmarked.

That is there are no buoys, no withies and unless your name is Harman you have absolutely no idea where the channel lies. True you can take a constitutional down the bank, jolly nice too, with the birds and the breeze, to spy out the lay of the land at low tide. And perhaps even take some bearings and draw, or was it be given, a little chart.

But come high water, it is just one brimming expanse of nothingness, flanked by sedge grass, with, as you know very well, glutinous mud lurking everywhere.

Invisibly, needless to say.

And in that strange way, high tide brought the usual knot of expectant faces, emerging from who knows where, in keen anticipation of someone else's misfortune, than which, as everybody knows, there is nothing more entertaining.

And one day it was our turn.

If you have an engine, as *Sauntress* then did, the prudent thing is to motor gingerly out with a firm eye on the echo sounder and the scrap of paper which does duty for a chart. But no, for there was a commanding breeze, the sun shone, the water glittered, and the notion formed that it would be fun to sail out.

So it was, but not for *Sauntress*.

First hoist the main, head to wind, and let go the lines. *Sauntress* paid off, gathered way and charged the nearest mudbank. Round one to the onlookers. Jane Harman appeared in the yard launch, which is pretty used to these occasions, was thrown a warp and towed us off, backwards, than which there is little more ignominious.

But there was more to come.

For *Sauntress*, mainsail now filling nicely, shot off down the creek, towing the yard launch backwards, Jane for some reason hanging on as the boatyard fast receded.

Thus giving the onlookers an unexpected bonus as Jane's frantic cries echoed across the water. But, you see I faced much the same dilemma as Gerard Hofnung's Bricklayer. If I let go the helm to let go Jane, we would run on the mud. But if I did not let go of Jane…?

So, like the bricklayer,

I hung on.

As did Jane.

The cottages shot past, the sedge grass shot past, the breeze strengthened. We negotiated the first bend, *Sauntress* picked up speed. Jane picked up volume and the show gave every sign of going on.

But, and here was the icing on the cake, the mainsheet became entangled with the helm and *Sauntress*, completely out of control, settled matters by ploughing to an abrupt halt in the mud.

Not so the yard launch.

Which, in the way of Newton and the apple...

Entertaining though the spectacle had been for the spectators, it said nothing for my ability to handle the ship, so what had gone wrong? Auxiliary engines make us lazy, but that was no excuse. And this, with hindsight was how the thing should have been done:

The head of the creek was scarcely a boat's length wide. The commanding breeze was blowing straight down the first section of the creek, which then curved to port, recurved to starboard, then port again and so on as far as Brightlingsea, where there would be room to manoeuvre. In short a run, a reach, a run, a reach and nothing on the wind.

If you forget about the engine you work as though it is not there. So instead of hoisting the main and casting off head to wind, thus pointing up the creek, where there was no chance at all of bearing away in the available space—for under main alone she will never pay off—I should first have warped the boat round to lie stern to wind. Something to be done quietly with no fuss or hurry, just let her swing.

Next, whilst the mainsail should be ready to be hoisted, with perhaps one tie to keep the sail tidy, and having made sure all runs clear, you leave it alone. Instead you unroll the foresail, but let the sheet run, so it is barely drawing. Now release your bow line, which will have been run round a post on the quay and brought back aboard, and tidy that away.

You are now secured only by the after warp, again round a post and brought back aboard. A quick check on the wind direction, a quick check that no-one is suddenly in the way and release the after warp, sheet in the foresail and the boat will slowly gather way, pointing down the creek, quite gently, for all you need is steerage way, giving you time to tidy away the aft warp and fenders.

As you swing round to port at the first turn, show a little main. That is to say you hoist the main so as to bring the luff taut, but leave the peak rucked away, bring in the mainsheet to avoid tangles, and the boat will reach comfortably, but not too fast on the short reach to the next turn.

Gybe her round that turn, getting the foresail across if necessary, all the time keeping way on, but no more than steerage way and in this fashion, with that commanding breeze, you ought to be able to get out.

Once out and with room, peak up the main, unroll the jib and away you go.

Needless to say, the procedure just described, or something like it, did not come as some sudden flash of enlightenment as I sat rather licking my wounded pride on the mooring in Pyefleet. It is what, a quarter of a century later, I would probably do if faced with the same situation again.

But one thing was clear, if there was to be no repetition it was high time I learned to handle the boat properly under sail.

And the quickest way to do that was to remove the engine.

Which that little incident brought just that much nearer.

9

On the Other Side

The sea reach of the Thames stretched before us like an interminable waterway. In the offing the sea and sky were welded together without a joint, and in the luminous space the tanned sails of the barges drifting up with the tide seemed to stand still in red clusters of canvas sharply peaked, with gleams of varnished sprits. A haze lay on the low shores that ran out to sea in vanishing flatness.

Joseph Conrad, *Heart of Darkness*.

THE STEADY CLANK, CLANK, CLANK which is cast iron pawl on cast iron ratchet can mean only one thing. The barge is bringing in her anchor. It is a sound absolutely unmistakable which carries over the still waters. For the Thames barge is a deliberate thing, steady, purposeful, unhurried, slowly swinging now as the wind takes hold and the wheel spins. Andy Harman looking aloft as he does so, judging from the pennant the slant of the wind, a glance aft, for he is watching too the set of the tide, a practised eye calculating distances, drift, speed, all those separate forces translated, into a few spokes of the wheel, this way or that, a sheet eased, or brought in as eighty feet and as many tons of engineless barge slips away on yet another voyage.

Someone will be walking slowly up the deck, for there must be no fuss or hurry in this, no shouting, and certainly no garish oilskins, for the uniform of the bargeman is a pair of overalls, maybe set off with a kerchief. An order will be given, another spoke of the wheel, and gathering way now, she heels imperceptibly to the south west breeze, bound for the Spitway and beyond, for it is time, once again for the Swale Match.

"Fancy a cup of tea George?"

George was a wonderful crew, strong, too strong at times, as he was famous for breaking things, competent, enthusiastic, crazy about fishing, crazy about birds, but George ran on tea like a car runs on petrol.

Whilst tea was making we shortened up on the anchor. The wind, SW 3-4 veering westerly later, was about as good as we could hope for, for the passage across the Thames to the Swale. The tide was beginning to make, the first signs of the scum of the flood beginning to cover the mud off Bateman's Wreck.

Now *Edme* was gone only the bawley *Helen and Violet* lay astern, and beyond that Pyefleet and our mooring. But we had dropped down to Bateman's the night before so as to be ready, as good an anchorage as you could wish for, tucked in behind Stone Point. Behind us, as *Sauntress* now turned to the tide, lay the marshes and the wildlife George adored, but today would need pilotage and careful working of the tides.

One reef in the main, *Sauntress* heeled to the breeze and set out in pursuit of *Edme*, by now off Inner Bench Head and holding her own nicely, lee-bowing as the tide poured up the Colne. We would be unlikely to catch her, but her silhouette would always be there ahead of us, for there was only one way to get to the Swale and that might politely be described as tortuous.

The depths in the Thames Estuary and the Kent and Essex rivers would give the blue water sailor nightmares. Four Fathom Channel is about as deep as you get. A few feet beneath the keel is comfortable and a few inches far from unknown.

Your path is barred by iron-hard sands, which cover and uncover; the tides run ferociously; wind over tide kicks up spiteful little waves; but almost in the way of a well-loved country lane the buoys, the beacons, the forts, give you your bearings and guide you safely through.

And so it was for us that day.

Out to Inner Bench Head, lee-bowing like *Edme*, ease the sheets a little for Colne Bar buoy, for now the west-going tide has got you, slip through the Wallet Spitway, two buoys to guide you through there, one ahead and one astern, for the tide will be setting you down if you are not careful, and your next mark is the Whittaker Beacon standing forlorn, most likely topped by a cormorant, five miles out from anywhere, marking the edge of the Foulness Sand.

"Got the fishing line Martin?"

"Yes George," a little wearily.

Still, you never know and occasionally George would catch a fish and not the log line.

"Another reef?"

"No, I think she can stand it."

Now we were butting our way down the Swin, Foulness and Maplin Sands to starboard, and another beacon to guide us, wary eye on the compass, another on the depth until…

"*Edme* has tacked."

She had, too.

"Better not to risk it George," and round we came for we had squeezed as close as we dared to the sands, and the smoothing of the water, as much as the depth sounder, told us we were quite close enough. This smoothing of the water is a little like that old adage 'smelling the sands,' for what that smoothing tells you is that there is less current here. And if there is less current here it is because you are out of the main channel or stream, closing the sands.

But the tide, three knots or so, was urging us on. Against us it would be a very different matter, an interminable beat to windward down the West Swin to reach South West Barrow, but as it was we could afford to pinch her and let the tide do its stealthy work.

"She's round Martin!"

And so she was, *Edme* now standing away south-east. George thought he had a bite, but no and at half flood we too rounded South West Barrow and eased the sheets for a romp in playful pursuit.

"Cup of tea George?"

(Must look after your crew).

Shivering Sands Towers, like great monsters out of the War of the Worlds, were our next and unmistakable mark.

"Look Martin, someone signalling."

A little off our starboard bow she was, apparently stopped, the solitary figure aboard waving in that unmistakable way. I recognised the boat, a tiny gaffer, valiantly sailed, but what could be the matter?

Engine trouble? A leak? Gear failure?

But no, he was lost.

All too easy. There was no GPS then. And if you fail to pick up your marks, fail to keep a log, you are potentially in serious trouble, for the banks are not visible. The estuary just looks like an enormous stretch of water and to blunder around blind is to invite disaster.

So we shortened sail and led her in to Spaniard.

Later, when we anchored in the Swale, it was not in splendid isolation, but amongst the biggest fleet of traditional craft to meet anywhere on the East Coast: Thames barges, bowsprit barges, staysail barges, restricted staysail barges, smacks, bawleys, Baltic traders, Dutch barges, historic power vessels, large large gaffers, large gaffers, small gaffers; and tomorrow we would race.

10

Dreaming?

N IGHT HAD LONG SINCE FALLEN.
　　Portland Bill lay astern in the darkness. *Sauntress* was whispering along. A caressing land breeze, no more. Away to starboard were the lights of some town, Lyme Regis most likely. Look back over your shoulder and there was Portland light, flashing 4 every 20 seconds. That impersonal leer which ought to be comforting but in fact only increases your sense of isolation.

And somewhere ahead lies the Devon coast, but you will not see that until dawn, supposing this wind holds. Further out to sea are the shipping lanes, the proverbial ships passing in the night, but they are too far away to bother you.

But here there is absolutely nothing, just you and your ship. You seek company in Richard Strauss, *The Four Last Songs*, but they serve only to accentuate the haunting solitude.

For you are single-handing.

Not some short coastal hop, but a passage which will last twenty-four, maybe thirty-six hours, no port of refuge, no-one to keep you company, share the watches, make a cup of tea, help reef the ship; in a way the ultimate drug and, like all drugs, dangerously addictive.

And deliberately you heighten the pathos, over and over and over again those *Four Last Songs*, as you savour the solitude, the velvet darkness, the apprehension, the sense of timelessness. And the boundary between the present, the past and the future begins to dissolve.

And now, of course you can begin to play with time.

Dismiss the humdrum.

Brest. What is Brest where we have been, are going, will go? Somehow it seems utterly irrelevant. What is relevant is the here and now, the uniqueness of this lone passage, forever engraved on your memory.

Will the little breeze hold?

Past midnight, when all the world is abed, the Shipping Forecast, must remember the Shipping Forecast, but before that, that night companion, the much loved tune, *Sailing By*; I wonder if they know? I wonder, I mean, if they think of those out there, like us, who are listening in the small hours. You find the pencil, a small torch, and wait.

General Synopsis at... How useful it would be to learn shorthand, damn, what did he say? But you get the gist, another low coming in. And how you detest the English Channel, with its perpetual headwinds, rapacious harbour-masters, horrible tides, but we did say we were going to Brest.

Or something.

No stars. No moon. The cloud must be rolling in.

But still the world holds its breath. Still the breeze holds. Still the Strauss.

And you know now that you must go further, much further, further and wilder and purer.

Dreaming.

As rosy fingered dawn...

11

The Swale Match

"CUP OF TEA GEORGIE?"
(George, by the way, would have described that night passage in rather more matter of fact terms.)

As days go it was a stinker. NE 6, rain, mist, and more of the same promised. A typical August snorter in short, with every possible ingredient, wind over falling tide, awful visibility, the place infested with mud banks; there was a touch of going over the top, with heavy casualties to be expected, or at least a tide spent on a mud bank, and to cap it all *Chittabob* was there.

For *Chittabob* meant one thing.

You hadn't a hope in hell.

This was a pursuit race, first round the course wins. And *Chittabob* being a 28-foot open day racer of 1913 vintage, an East Coast One Design, she was fast in her own right, but with Arthur Keeble, a kind of mischievous living legend, at the helm, utterly unbeatable.

But you had to respect the man. The boat might well be fast, indeed blindingly so, but she had a huge open well, heavy lead keel, leaked like a sieve in a seaway and, should she take a sea green, glug, glug. So she needed nursing in these conditions.

And Arthur Keeble always single-handed.

With Georgie making sheep's eyes at the wildlife and the mudflats, for he did not think much of this racing lark, and bolstered by his cuppa, we prepared for the race. With, unless the log lies, but why should it, full main and topsail, an idiotic rig in the circumstances. Blood up, nostrils flaring, away, grossly over-canvassed we went.

The casualties, you saw them out of the corner of your eye on the mudflats, were not long in coming; we rounded South Girdler with *Edme* and *Portlight*, thundering would be the word, to windward. And you do not, but absolutely not, try your luck with a Thames Barge on full song, by doing something as stupid as shouting for water at the mark.

Ease the sheets in the direction of what you hope is the Herne Bay mark, for you can see absolutely nothing in the mist, find it, more by luck than judgement, follow the leader not being a good idea as most probably they have no more idea than you. And onto a run where the wind fails and we are treated to a Wagnerian thunder-and-lightning downpour to drift, six and three quarter hours later, across the line.

To complete, as the Match report records, "a thundering good race."

And after the race a long and riotous night after the prize-giving in the boat shed. Essex Raiders, Men of Kent, little needle matches here and there, the odd leg pulled, someone for sure a muddy ducking.

And see you next year?

What preserves the atmosphere of these remote places, and Hollowshore is certainly remote, is that the creeks creep inland through the saltings, water merging with mud, merging in turn with sedge grass, so that anything in the way of houses is kept so far distant as to be invisible.

The boat shed was just that, a kind of replica Toosey on the other side, a big cavernous place hung with oars, sails and all the paraphernalia of traditional boats.

In the creek outside, the drying mud berths, next door a pub and apart from that nothing but water and sky, wide open sky over the flatlands, wind in the winter that cuts like a knife, a scene, in short, that Conrad's Marlowe would recognise.

And yes, one year Arthur Keeble was not there, which is how we fly, on special days, the coveted Swale Match Pennant.

The name of the Kentish Sail Association Journal?

On the Mud.

And that, Georgie, is why the Swale knocks spots off Brest.

12

Less is More

"YOU DON'T HAVE AN ENGINE, DO YOU?"
"No."
"I can always tell. Your sails set beautifully."

And that, of course is the point. You are quite entitled to say that to remove a perfectly good Japanese auxiliary engine from *Sauntress* is an act bordering on madness. And so it may be.

But it was done, and once done was rather like having a tooth out. You feel so much better. And so indeed did *Sauntress*. Always nimble, she positively danced for joy. "Like silk," said Crispin as he took the helm. And it was rather like removing a ball and chain from a haggard prisoner. She came alive.

But at a price. Called experience.

The mooring in Pyefleet was a constant delight. You were (yet again) with the birds, the mud flats, those wide East Anglian skies, 'pick your own' just up the lane, the key to the gate, the dinghy waiting, oars underneath, the Kerrisons in their eyrie in the shape of the Colchester Oyster Fishery, with a friendly eye on the moorings, and little else.

And what now did the ship need? Water, food, paraffin for the lamps, charcoal for the heater, tender loving care and nothing else. Autumn, then winter drew in. Still *Sauntress* sailed. The charcoal stove glowed. Oil lamps threw their friendly shadows, frost on the decks. And oh the migrating birds. Georgie would have known them all. And how evocative those haunting cries, or sometimes a shriek in the night. Or a seal popping inquisitive nose. And a great gibbous moon above.

Winter sailing. There is nothing like it.

Except...

One of those silvery days. A hazy winter sun. A faint breeze. We slipped, as so many times, the mooring, the we being *Sauntress* and her skipper, as one now, for a little sail, nothing ambitious, poke our nose into Brightlingsea, "to be admired" says the log with proper conceit, adding enigmatically "admired JL."

Who precisely is JL?

Answer James (Jimmy) Lawrence, an East Coast Institution, if ever there were one. There are of course delightful rivalries and undercurrents in the relatively small world of the Essex rivers, but when it came to sail-making for smacks, bawleys and little gaffers like us, James Lawrence was the name on all lips. For he is, it must be said, a consummate showman. One of those figures very sure of their place in the scheme of things, dripping with what might be called local colour, he had made our first suit of sails.

But there were of course rumblings of rebellion here and there; another sail-maker had erupted on the scene, rather pointedly winning the Swale match, and there was Gowen's up the proverbial road, not the obvious choice for the strictly traditional brigade.

And it was their sails he was admiring.

Preening the feathers somewhat, for who does not when their ship is admired, we wafted back across the Colne, past *Helen and Violet*, past the Colchester Oyster Fishery, past the moorings, bound for the head of the creek for one of those nights at anchor.

It was not to be. A moment's lapse in concentration and *Sauntress* gybed and ploughed sedately to a halt in the mud. That would not matter except that it was the very top of the tide, the wind, or what there was of it, was onshore and the tides were, as the saying goes, taking off. Thus there was every chance of being ignominiously neaped. But not if I could help it, for rule number one in this game is self-reliance, no accepting tows, no weakly giving in, though exactly how I was going to get her off again was a bit of a puzzle.

The log makes bleak reading. Attempts to kedge her off that evening came to nothing. She was stuck for the night, and a long night it was to be, jammed as I was at an angle, listening to the wind moaning, speculating on my chances.

"Awake at 1 o'clock, start preparing, slow at night with wind now piped up and quite strong, making putting two reefs in the main a slow business, get it right eventually, change foresail, wind now 5 plus, High Water, *Sauntress* pitching in her hole but sticking, pointing shoreward." Still hauling on the kedge, but plainly this is not enough. She just will not budge. There is less water on this tide. And defeat staring bleakly.

Then there came a flash of somewhat belated inspiration. Up went the foresail. Up went the big James Lawrence jib and to hell with the strain. Both backed. Reluctantly *Sauntress* began to turn in her mud bed until we had the wind fine on the starboard quarter. At least the boat was now pointing into deep water, but it was still not enough and the tide was beginning to run off.

So up with a struggle went the double-reefed main, pinned as it was against the shrouds. And now the force of the wind told. *Sauntress* heeled, main sheeted in, headsails backed, she heeled still further, more power now than any engine, never mind kedge, until reluctantly the mud released its grip and suddenly, heaven be praised, she came clear.

Perspiring profusely, yet chilled to the marrow, the lazy wind as they call it hereabouts cutting like the proverbial knife, there was work yet, for we lay in 18in of water on a falling tide with no time to be lost. Conditions the smacks-men on their winter fishing grounds would know only too well, snow-laden sky, frozen hands hauling on wet and rough lines, salt in the wounds; but the ship comes first, and so it was that morning.

Haul in the kedge until almost up-and-down. Chuck aside the useless and sodden gloves in disgust. Back the foresail to break the kedge out, let fly the sheet, gather steerage way, tack again for the creek is narrow and the tide running off, heave her to a moment to get in the anchor, tack again and so on, ever colder until the mooring is reached.

Nobody is about on this bitter February morn. The wind against tide is kicking up a fearsome little sea even here in the creek, all feeling is gone from the fingers, fumble the mooring, fumble again and lose the boat-hook and in sheer desperation heave to, drift down on the darned thing, grab it and jam it behind the shrouds.

Now you can get a line to the bitts, and thence through the eye on the buoy, make the ship tidy, stow the sails, and at last, when all is done, you may light the stove and begin to thaw out.

"Utterly spent but quietly triumphant," reads the log, for we had done it and done it alone.

13

Nothing Ventured

Sailing without an engine is much more fun.
—Humphrey Barton, *Vertue* XXXV

"YOU NEED A PAIR OF SWEEPS."
The speaker is Richard Woodman, a man to be reckoned with in Harwich, whose kindly eye fell on *Sauntress*. And by some sleight of hand a pair of beautiful sweeps materialised, with the unspoken implication that it was time to learn new skills.

"Sculled out" read the log, in deference, naturally to Richard Woodman.

And a new kind of entry appeared:

"Fox Bottom to Osea Crew George.

0600 Fog. No wind.

1000 No fog, sun, no wind.

But George cooks a delicious breakfast and we reflect on the joys of waiting for the wind."

And there was no irony in the joys. The nettle had been grasped and the rewards were being reaped. *Sauntress* at last had come of age. There is a rather curious adage, less is more. But it is apt. The more things were stripped away, the better she handled, faster, nimbler, sweeter, and above all more fun to sail.

"She looked magnificent, showed us all up," wrote Jon.

Yup, Jon Wainwright, he of the slippery-as-an-eel *Deva*, one of those boats which may not look much, but just wait and see her go. And Jon was never one for head-of-the-creek solitude; a beer, a good laugh and plenty of committee work was more in his line. But he loved that boat and wrote of his love, *Only So Many Tides* it is called, prophetic that, for like McMullen before him, he died at the helm.

So if he paid you a compliment you took it at face value.

And those committees?

The Old Gaffers Association, East Coast Chapter, for it was a tight little world was that. But without them no rallies, no races, no fun and games at Shotley.

Oh dear, Shotley.

For quite a few years, for a whole long week came the Shotley Festival. And Shotley, God help us, was a marina, into which and out of which every day one had to lock. And that with no engine was certainly interesting. But as it turned out quite manageable. And, festival within a festival, the Peter Pan and Wendy combination, being Crispin and Edith, presented such awards as

The Award of the Golden Whip
To Martin
for
Being a hard Captain with an unruly crew
presented by
Nancy Blackett   U.P. Anchor

The Skipper came down and took his shoes off.

"Aren't you going to undress?" said Roger.

"No" said Jim.

"Gosh" said Roger.

Gosh indeed.

But what about those wilder shores?

14

The Wilder Shores

OST OF US WHO SAIL IN THE OLD WAY have our mariner's
library. Where, when the winters' gales wuther (as they say in York-
shire) around the eaves, we lose ourselves, by a flickering fire, in accounts of
voyages of which we can only dream.

And amongst all these, the Slocums, the O'Briens, the Smeetons and
countless others, lies buried a little gem, which in its modesty and simplicity touched a particular chord. It is called *The Adventure of the Faroe
Islands*, written by the daughter of Commander Graham, Helen. And
it appears as a kind of appendix to his much greater adventure *Rough
Passage*, with foreword by none other than our old friend Claud Worth. Graham's boat, *Emanuel*, is engineless, and the year 1929:

Racing along at 6 knots, course north, up the Irish Sea.

We anchored in Loch Don and went ashore for milk, which we were
very kindly given, the cow being specially milked for us. We obtained a
lovely view over the Lochs, the purple heather-clad mountain tops ton-
ing down through all shades to the vivid blue of the water below.

Mate [being Helen Graham] instructed in the use of the sextant,
but would use the index glass as a mirror in which to admire herself.

[And why not?]

Some fishermen said we were mad, or at least implied it, to think of
going to the Faeroes.

"Shall we go on?" asked the skipper

"Rather," I replied and so we went on.

Not only mischievous, but stout-hearted.

And that little tale, so innocently told, gave the key. If we were to escape the crowds, find a little adventure and those proverbial wilder shores, we had to go north, not south; to icy waters, iron-bound coasts, the land of the midnight sun. In short, Norway.

Six hundred and fifty nautical miles distant, exactly the kind of little challenge that Georgie relished. We had the ship, we had the time and we had the crew. So we went.

23rd June Day 2. Wind NW 3-4 occasionally 5.

"Crash, bash, swell and cross swell," reads the log as we reel off the miles steadily. Where we are is another matter as the GPS refuses to give a position, but as there is plenty of sea room there seems little point in worrying. The wetness is rather tiresome. At intervals *Sauntress* buries her bowsprit and scoops up a wave over the bow which comes foaming back over the coachroof and pouring into the cockpit, or the cabin if we have left the hatch open. Leaks appear in all sorts of places, especially over our bunks, which are getting wetter and wetter, as are we. A check on the lee rigging reveals two shackles have undone themselves and are about to let go, the cap-shroud and starboard bowsprit stay. Both are tightened and wired."

The North Sea may not look much in the scheme of things, but believe me, it has a temper. And that temper, as we cleared Orford Ness, made itself felt in the shape of an unexpected NW swell, with nasty cross seas, into which *Sauntress* butted wetly and none too happily. And it lost no time in finding out the weaknesses: the shackles I had failed to wire, the leaks I had chosen to ignore, the stowage which summers on the East Coast had made a little lazy. But we had plenty of sea room. And there is the key. For we had elected not to go creeping timidly from port to port, but boldly, lay off the course for Norway and sail it. For sea room, in any yacht, but certainly one with no engine, is a luxury, a sense of comfort, for it is land which sinks boats, not, as a general rule, the sea.

Log now 168. Daily distance run 83 miles.

24 June Day 3. Wind N becoming variable 3.

"Time. 0530. Wind Direction/force. NW4. Visibility. Good. Course 025. Log. 168 Tidal set/leeway none. DR/fix Petro 5. Other. Yellow buoy. And so on, hour after hour, day after day. The deck log which records where we are, or think we are, how far we have gone, what the wind is doing, the course, the time, the log reading. For with that you can reconstruct. And without it you are lost, literally, particularly given the entry, "GPS still sulking.""

25th June Day 4. Forecast SW 3 veering NW 4-5.

"Morning coffee and toast, (and how one longs for that), interrupted by a large freighter which having passed astern startles me by reappearing on our starboard beam, stopped. Fairly plainly she is taking an interest so I wave and try to look unconcerned, sure that powerful binoculars are trained on us. After about 15 minutes she sets off on her way. GPS finally consents to work giving us a position 54.41.35N by 05.28.93.E at 0810, which is close enough to our estimated position to be respectable. Log 314.6. Distance run 76 miles.

But how bizarre that a big freighter, about its lawful ways, should ring down the engines to stop and lie off our beam! It is a lovely peaceful morning. We are slipping along in good order. There is nothing in the forecast to cause concern. Yet there she is, stopped, a few cables off.

A mystery never solved, but it happened again.

26 June. Day 5. Forecast SW 3-4.

"We enjoy a truly fabulous sunset. Log 430. Distance run. 116 miles. An uneventful day of fast sailing."

27 June. Day 6. Forecast NW 4-5.

"Amazing sunrise," reads the log entry.

"The wind which has veered NW is now strengthening quickly. We furl the jib and put the second reef in the main. The wind increases further and the waves get larger, reaching a size where in the trough the horizon is the next wave whilst on the crests a tumbling and foam-streaked vista greets the eyes. On watch one spends the time dodging the spray. Below the noise is horrible as one heart-stopping crash follows another. Finally we decide enough is enough and heave to. She lies quietly. A trawler comes and inspects us, lying off our port quarter for a while. We lie hove to for the next 12 hours. Quite glad of a rest. Log 480. Distance run. 59 miles. Position 52.27.58N by 5.45.32.E at 2025."

This is the third time a ship has diverted to have a look at us with, we assume, friendly intent. Which, whilst comforting in a way, suggests that the sight of a gaff cutter way out in the wastes of the North Sea, with its occasionally savage, as now, moods, is so unusual now as to excite, perhaps curiosity, as well as just checking that all is well. As before, we wave and they move off,

28 June. Day 7. Forecast NW backing SE 3-4 occasionally 5.

"What do you eat?"

Answer, today ratatouille "delicious even without garlic," for we are well provisioned, especially with tea. Which Georgie consumes endlessly. Log 551. Distance run 68. Miles. Lights twinkle on the Norwegian coast. Position 58.13. 36N by 5.56.21E at 2000. (The GPS only works when there is little movement).

29 June. Day 8 Forecast SE 5 becoming variable 4.

"A wild night," reads the log. The second in three days as the wind rapidly rises, we put in all three reefs, tearing away downwind on a run and *Sauntress* practically unmanageable. "A violent and heart stopping gybe decides matter. The main must come down. This gave us some anxious moments. Smothering the sail was no easy matter. George, hanging onto the boom, tying the ties, was flung from one side of the cockpit to the other, each time suspended over the water, whilst I hung onto his waist."

Rather clunky prose for what was in all conscience a very nasty time. By a mercy the involuntary gybe carried nothing away. Take the main off a boat in a seaway and she rolls wickedly. The wind is doing its banshee act. It is pitch black. We cling on for dear life. And you wonder, really, just what else is going to happen. To Georgie, whose imagination runs along other lines, this is just another little tussle in the night, all in a day's, or in this case a night's, work. Very reassuring crew was Georgie. And if he broke things, not knowing his own strength, well, they should be stronger. But on this trip we broke nothing, not even a lamp chimney.

"The wind went and so did the visibility."

For the summer squall, vicious whilst it lasted, blew itself out. Now farm-yard smells, more pungent to salt-filled nostrils, spoke of our promised land. And it was different up here, even at sea. "But the colour of the waves is the thing, the palest icy blue," read the log entry the day we hove to in the storm. So no, we cannot have been frightened, still less in any danger, just sick of punishing the boat and ourselves. For hove to we could rest, doze, eat, ob-serve and wait for things to settle down. And marvel at the purest ice blue waves.

Our old friend sea room again.

A long-keeled boat like *Sauntress* will heave to easily. I had never tried it at sea in such conditions as these, but she behaved as she always behaved, foresail backed, main sheeted out a touch, tiller lashed a little to leeward. The transformation when you stop bashing your and the ships' brains out in a futile thrash to windward is remarkable. The wind is just the same, but now the boat, instead of fighting it, lies quietly, drifting slowly to leeward, completely under control, for you have only to ease the foresail again to be sailing. Meantime you may rest, have a cuppa, study the chart, make a stew and generally take a break. A much underestimated art. And if we lost 12 miles, what did that matter in a passage of 650 or more.

It's not the ships. It's the men in them, as the old saying goes.

30 June. Day 9. Variable 3 or 4. Fog.

All wind went. A clammy fog closed in, and siren-like those farmyard smells lured *Sauntress* shore-ward. Out at sea the wraith-like forms of large ships would appear and disappear, shore traffic up the Norway coast, the steady thump, thump of engines rather sinister in the prevailing gloom. Rocks appeared to starboard, fangs, no doubt they ought to be called, lying in wait for the unwary, for we were caught, slightly between the devil of the reefs and the not so deep blue sea in the shape of those blind monsters, thump, thump, thump, for it would not do to mix with them. So we drifted, rested, and waited, 28 miles in 24 hours.

"North Utsire, South Utsire, Forties, Cromarty, Forth…" drones the Shipping Forecast

Ever wondered about those Utsires? I know I have. Surprise. Utsire is an island and the dawn fix showed we were running it down. For suddenly, or reasonably suddenly given our stately pace of 1 knot, rocks appeared over the bow, so we hauled round westwards. More rocks! Reversed course and tail between the legs headed back the way we came before heading out to sea again, not a little frightened by the blunder. Then the wind returned, NW by W, the skies cleared and we scurried thankfully clear.

It was to be our last night at sea.

The higher the latitude, the more spectacular the sunset. And this one was without question the crowning glory, leaving us groping for superlatives, entranced at the display. But as the last colour faded, the moon took centre stage, for it was a full moon and not just a full moon, but a blue moon into the bargain.

Damp, tired, dirty we might be, but all that, and watch-keeping too was forgotten for we both knew we would never see anything quite like it again, the spectacle for which those on cruise ships pay a fortune, but we were not on a cruise ship, we were aboard *Sauntress*, reaping the reward for our rashness, than which there is nothing sweeter.

'Madame la lune' as the incantation goes, mother of the tides, drawer of sap, the subject of countless proverbs and sayings, at which wolves howl, from which the very word lunatic derives, in the light of which the crew of a square-rigger in the tropics would never, but never sleep, 'moonshine moves tides, why not faces' quotes Eric Newby in The Last Grain Race, the moon is a thing of power, mystery and inspiration.

And if I regretted then and regret now that I was too late for the old square-riggers, a mood the same author captures perfectly in this quotation, aboard *Moshulu*, in 1938, 'down to topsails now, her upper and lower yards naked, gleaming yellow like bones in the moonlight, she was a terrible wild stranger to us. At the wheel a Dane and a Swede were fighting to hold her as she ran at thirteen and fourteen knots in the gusts. I knew then I would never see sailing like this again. When ships such as this went it would be the finish.'

Whether it was that quotation, or the full moon, or both, I firmly believe that on that night a seed was planted, one that took years to germinate, and its name, perhaps you can guess, was the square-sail.

For one hundred years earlier almost to the day, in the very same latitude, a youth called Claud Worth in a yacht scarcely bigger than *Sauntress* was at sea under just such a sail.

That, if you wish to see it so, is the power of the moon.

15

Norwegian Strawberries

1 July. Day 10.

ADMIRALTY PILOT IN HAND we compared the mountainous coast with the sketch, "approach to Korsfjorden from W, in two views, with Marstein light."

There could be no doubt. The lighthouse showed whitely in a brief ray of sunshine.

10 miles to go.

"At 0800 log 672 Marstein bears E ½ mile. Hand log."

"We enter the Fjord. The motion ceases and we sail on with a gentle beam wind, full of curiosity."

We have reached our wilder shores.

Our arrival we celebrate by sleeping for sixteen hours.

Georgie loses no time in befriending two small boys, discussing fishing. In what language heaven knows, for we have no Norwegian and they no English. They inspect *Sauntress* and return later with a small gift, a tray of homemade chocolates.

For the time being we rest. George must go home and Crispin is due. It was time to consult the pilots and make plans. Any book which starts schoolmaster-like with "you must have a good engine," and how arrogant is that "must," and then warbles on about culture is a waste of space. Indeed a downright affront. So it went. The next tome was little better, so that too went.

That left the much derided, only for big ships, *Admiralty Pilot, Norway Pilot, Volume IIA, West Coast of Norway from Lindesnes to Stattlandet*. It contains sailing directions for entering the Fjords and sailing in them, and every possible anchorage and harbour is listed, with directions, comments on depths, holding and other relevant pilotage notes. One had simply to choose a likely spot on the chart, look it up in the pilot and read it up. It was invaluable. And not surprisingly, for this is the distilled wisdom of the British Navy over many, many years, and much of it under sail. And thus much more relevant to us.

So much so, that wherever *Sauntress* went on her subsequent travels, wilder shores, usually, the beloved Admiral came with us. It also has the irresistible phrase,

Small vessels with local knowledge may…

And that, of course meant, us.

Small vessels can anchor in Stronevag on the East side of Strono 3/4 mile NNE of Husfjelltangen…

Thus we crept our way, in thick mist and almost no wind, through this rock-infested, but not as bad as that, little gulf, to anchor, bower and fisherman, in 30 foot at the head of the very pine-clad creek the Admiral had so helpfully identified. No other yachts, no habitation, but a waterfall. Crispin goes ashore to explore.

Lokksund leads 5 miles south and connects Bjornafjordan with Ytre (outer) Hardanger. Its narrowest part is one cable wide.

We will not, it is clear have time to visit umpteen different fjords. But why should that matter? We are not 'doing' Norway in the way the Americans used to 'do' Europe. We have what we have come for, fabulous scenery, wonderful food, for we munch the delicious Norwegian bacon and equally delicious bread and we glide, in the sunshine at last, to try our luck with Lokksund, the five mile extremely narrow little passage to our next anchorage beyond.

And sufficient unto the day.

Lokksund, narrow and long, hemmed in by hills, like a mountain pass, with a little water at the bottom, lay ahead of us. It seemed most unlikely we would carry our wind, still less that we would sail free, for it had all the mak-

ings of a place of squalls, calms and violent wind shifts. For once however, such gloomy prognostications were wrong. We slipped through as if drawn by some invisible wire, raced, to our amusement and theirs, by a four man gig, the only craft at sea that day. We were entranced.

"Where next Crispin? Have a look at the Admiral will you?"

"How does this sound?" said Crispin after a short struggle with the index and the place names. He read aloud

Small vessels with local knowledge can anchor in a cove off Uskedal, close south of Flatholmen.

"See, just here, behind those islands" he added, pointing at the chart.

"Good, just give me the course will you?"

It was not really necessary. The islands lay over the bow five miles distant, on the other side of the Hardangerfjord as clear as could be, but only yesterday we had been groping around in the murk, so it seemed wiser to take no chances.

The log takes over.

"Near perfect sail, sun, calm sea, favourable wind, even through Lokksund and magnificent scenery all around. Two anchors down here, not so much because we fear a storm, as because I had anchored closer to the shore than I had meant to. We row out the fisherman in the dinghy and drop the anchor into the depths before shortening up. It dug in superbly as we discovered on leaving. And a pretty much perfect anchorage. We are tucked into the North East corner of a tiny bay, lying to two anchors in 10'. To windward is a further screen of islands and to leeward, the village, pastures and massive hills."

"Why," we asked a visiting Norwegian, who had rowed out to inspect, "is nobody sailing here?"

"The Germans," he answered, and how he spat the word, "only come in good weather." Adding, with what might have been a wink,

"Gales tomorrow."

Small craft may anchor in Kalvasund between the NE end of Snilsveitoy and Kalven.

Uskedalen to Kalven S veering W 6 to gale 8.

The channel is notorious for heavy mountain squalls.

Cow bells.

You could hear them tinkling somewhere up in the pastures. Tides were negligible. The place proliferated, thanks to our friend the Admiral, with tiny anchorages, always alone. The pilotage, through narrow winding channels, peppered with rocks, was just interesting enough to save it from being dull. And now and again the forecast wind would suddenly blow home. Much as we would have liked to stay and listen to our Norwegian and his probably hair-raising stories of the German occupation, we felt it more discreet, forecast gale 8 or no, to move on.

The Admiral was right about the squalls, but we had a bare three miles to sail, which we did either sitting looking at our own reflection, or lee rail under in a welter of foam. We wriggled into the anchorage, there being several rocks in the fairway. And here, weather-bound we stayed two days.

Not quite in the land of the midnight sun, but at 60°N, mid-summer permanent twilight. The same latitude as the Shetland Islands. To the sole accompaniment of Artic Terns.

These lovely black-capped birds, (Latin name *Sterna Paradisea*) with their forked tails and swept back wings, are reputed, rightly, to be quite extraordinarily aggressive. We watched as a gull, swimming around minding its own business, was subjected to an attack by half a dozen Arctic Terns dive bombing the luckless bird, which ducked, pathetically and ineffectually, for by the time the Terns had finished it was incapable of flight, either actual or metaphorical.

And their incessant screech, for you could not call it a song, made sleep nigh impossible. But every paradise has its serpent, in this case a winged one.

Ashore the second morning with water cans. There was a tiny wooden-floored store. "Might we have some water?" our needs being simple. The woman disappeared with the cans and returned with them filled from a stream. For there was no running water on this island. We bought a few provisions and left.

Kalven to Akresvag. W veering NW 5-6 occasionally 7 later.

Another simple passage. We drifted in for lunch and liked the place so much that we stayed. Crispin had arrived, rather like Carruthers aboard the *Dulcibella*, with a kind of lurid yellow portmanteau which was with difficulty accommodated below. This contained photographic equipment. And to give some purpose to this idyll, it was decreed we should visit a glacier. It should have been today, but tomorrow will do. Crispin ashore.

He returns with mussels for supper.

And had we accepted that half-extended invitation from that solemn old Norwegian, resting on his oars? Boatsheds and illegal stills abound. And from there a short step, a smoky cabin isolated in the woods, Akvavit, toast after toast, stories tumbling out, a kind of catharsis, closed communities, long harsh winters, memory, so much memory and to whom do you confide all this?

The stranger at the door.

For by morn he will be gone and your secrets with him.

Akresvag to Kobbevik and Sild. NW 5-6 decreasing 4.

Akrehamn or akresvag affords good anchorage to small vessels with localknowledge in depths from 7m to 10m mud. There are mooring rings on a skerry on the W side of the cove. The deepest entrance is E of the two skerries which lie close to the W side of Akreholmen; the entrance N of the islet has a depth of 5m over a rock close N of an iron perch marking a rock near the islet.

For once we were defeated. We were bound for Sundal in the Mauresfjord, a majestic glowering kind of place, where, says the Admiral you should watch out for rock falls and violent squalls. For this village lies at the foot of the glacier, up which Crispin proposed to scramble. The wind died. And we sat motionless, waiting for something to happen, maybe a rock fall, or a squall, to the accompaniment of the thunder of a waterfall.

But we had the sweep and this gave us a knot or so, and thus we reached a small anchorage for lunch. The wind turned onshore and we had a tricky moment getting clear, where a breeze took us to an island in the middle of the Fjord, called Sild.

A minor paradise. Quite safe. And those lovely delicate alpines which flower so briefly in these northern lands, where it seems a pity even to tread, so delicate and beautiful are they, growing in a bed of velvety and springy green moss.

"We spotted a pair of herons circling the anchorage, very graceful."

They were Alpines.

And rather, to use a metaphor, as you sit in a wood, waiting, senses heightened whilst you lose yourself in a kind of infinite patience, so, slowly does the wood begin to talk. Faintly at first and then, as you allow all else to fade away, so a thousand voices begin to speak.

And so it was here.

But snap a twig and they are gone.

To have had, never mind used an engine in this wilderness would have been akin to sacrilege. Once a hydrofoil thundered by, leaving us rolling in its wake, the noise reverberating from mountain to mountain long after it had gone. Then a kind of primeval peace returned and we could glide silently on, for *Sauntress* had found what she had come looking for, those longed-for wilder shores.

On the last night and for the very first time, we dined ashore, very formally, *Sauntress* on the quay below, a creamed fish soup with mussels, roast reindeer and, insisted our demure waitress in a waisted green outfit straight out of The Sound of Music, with accent to match, "please try them. They are delicious" Norwegian Strawberries.

Tushen tat, said we, for that in Norwegian means

Thank you.

16

In the Little Downs

THE ANCHOR CHAIN RATTLED OUT. *Sauntress* swung to the tide and we were at rest. It was strangely peaceful after all the commotion off Dover, the snarling hovercraft, the impatient ferries, the bleak view to windward as a strong south westerly wind fought with the four knot tide, short curling waves, pump dismantled, too much water in the bilges. The struggle to get clear of Dover had become pointless, so we ran back to anchor in the Little Downs.

We had McMullen to thank for that. For those old books do not just entertain. They instruct. Infinitely preferable to the ghastliness of Dover, or the dubious delights of Ramsgate, we lay quite peacefully protected by the bulk of the South Foreland off the open beach and here, as long as the wind stayed south west, we could remain.

Night fell. To seaward the myriad buoys marking the Goodwins winked in the darkness, Ramsgate was a blaze of light, the sea murmured on the shingle and no-one disturbed us. The bobstay tackle slackened off, the chain looped over the fairlead, we would lie quiet as *Sauntress* ranged on her anchor.

"Happy Georgie?"

"Yes."

For Georgie being Georgie, no sooner was the anchor down than he was busy with bearings, noted in the log, and for the rest of the afternoon he had been checking to be sure they had not changed. But the anchor was well dug in. Two reefs in the main, jib and foresail ready furled on the Wykeham-Martin gear, we could be under way at a moment's notice. And unlikely though that seemed, it was as well to be prepared.

When last did a yacht lie here?

The old barges, Oh yes, I remembered those. And how suddenly, like a flock of starlings, when the slant came, they would make sail as one, and the Little Downs would be empty again.

Supper cleared away, *Sauntress* rolling rhythmically, the waves murmuring on the beach, oil lamps lit, tomorrow's tides checked, Georgie snoring like a walrus up forward (making sleep impossible), there was time to reflect.

There is a line, a very fine line, between what might be called legitimate adventure, or sport, and recklessness, the foolhardy taking of risks. And to remove the auxiliary engine from *Sauntress* and with it a certain margin of safety, took us that much closer to that line. Yet Georgie came, Crispin came and not just once, but time after time. And that they would not do that if they thought the thing foolhardy. Both were experienced, both had their own boats and seldom, if ever did they comment on the eccentricity of the skipper in his search for… what?

The answer is simply given. If our forebears could do it, why not we? We have grown soft (a little voice said), too soft. Where are the skills they took for granted? Turn the pages of Claud Worth or Maurice Griffiths or, to come closer to home, E.F. Knight: neither snow nor ice, nor leaky ships stopped them. There was zest and real adventure. But the world has changed (another little voice says). Yes it has, out of all recognition, you reply, but the sea is the same, the yacht you sail is, as it happens, the same. And the techniques are the same, albeit almost forgotten.

Thus their skills become your skills. Where they scull, you scull. Where they anchored, you anchor. Where they run on the mud, you run on the mud. And much more importantly get yourself off again. And that was the reason for the "utterly spent, but quietly triumphant" in Pyefleet creek that bitter February day.

For to have failed then would have been a humiliation beyond bearing.

The anchor chain grumbled. Turn of the tide.

17

Down Channel

"READY ABOUT?"
A pause,
"Lee Ho!"

Sauntress came through the eye of the wind and, jib and foresail sheeted in, stood off the land again, wind SW force 4 maybe 5, working her way steadily to windward, two reefs in the main, sailing a little free in the short lumpy seas.

What no winches?

No sir, we had them once but they were a pest. The sheets jammed, or worse, leapt the drum to disappear in a flash up forward to be flogged into an insane tangle, neither good for the sail nor your seamanship.

Jamming cleats proved the answer, sheets led through openings in the coaming and then knotted, figure of eight. You had to be quick but that was hardly a hardship, no sooner than through the eye of the wind, sheet in and you are away, silent, simple and effective.

Dungeness lay upwind, maybe five miles. The tide which had swept us, on a rather switchback ride, past Dover, Folkestone and other such places, was about to turn. And at two or three knots against us, that meant six hours going nowhere much.

But there was Dungeness roads, not to anchor, as off Deal, though it is a recognised anchorage, but a place out of the tide, shallow and calm waters, where we could sneak up on Dungeness and take the place, so to speak, by surprise. George disapproved of what to the skipper was a perfectly sensible idea, learned in racing, seek the back-eddy, but was over-ruled.

It does not do to have two skippers on one boat.

The logic was impeccable. A lee shore one avoids like the plague. But this was not a lee shore. It was a weather shore. Freed from waves and tide, sheets eased, *Sauntress* picked up her skirts and went, shot back into the maelstrom that was the tide off Dungeness point, having gained several miles, and broke free.

Stand off the land until the shipping lanes, tack back in again, stand off the land, but we were three, not two, George, Crispin and the skipper. And that meant companionship on the long night watches, *Sauntress* with a line over the tiller more or less sailing herself to windward, stand off the land until the shipping lanes, tack back in again…

"You did not like Holland, did you Martin?"

"No, Crispin, I did not."

"Why?"

"You have read *The Riddle of the Sands*, haven't you?"

That was not a question which needed asking, for who, who owns a gaff rigged yacht, has not read and re-read that wonderful book?

"He puts it rather well. You remember Davies is talking to Carruthers about his passage out from England, I think I can quote from memory."

"*Like fools we decided to go through Holland by the canals… it was a wretched business, nothing but paying lock dues, bumping against schuyts and towing down stinking canals. Never a peaceful night, always moored by some quay, people passing, boys throwing stones.*"

He is absolutely right. It is still like that, even down to the boys throwing stones, except, for boys, read drunken adults throwing bottles. Each to his own it must be said, but if you like the wilder shores, the lonely creeks, the cries of the birds, Holland is not for you.

At last the south-westerly wind went, leaving us becalmed somewhere off the Dorset coast, St Albans and the Needles lights visible off the starboard quarter, *Sauntress* immobile on a glassy sea, waiting for a new wind. Senses heightened as they are in the absolute stillness, a sudden rushing in the water startled, indeed a moment of irrational fear. A monster of the deep you might call it, but Georgie, more pragmatically, pronounced "probably basking shark."

The wind returned, from the east this time and by mid-morning, Portland Bill astern, *Sauntress* was tacking downwind in fine style, bowsprit kissing the troughs as we surged on the crests of the waves.

Tacking downwind sounds nonsensical but it is not. A gaff-rigged vessel on a dead run is a handful and should you have the bad luck to gybe all standing, you are quite likely to break something or brain the crew. So we put the wind on the quarter until the foresail and jib filled and in this fashion, crisscrossing your true course, you are safer and faster.

Dartmouth of not so happy memory beckoned once more, a forecast SW7 having decided matters, and by nightfall we were in the river, listening to the crack of doom, as the mother and father of thunderstorms echoed down the valley.

On passage, Dartmouth to Falmouth. Crew George. June 1999.

"Whispering along, a night breeze off the land, a starlit sky above and dark brooding headlands as far as the eye could see. No waves here, just wavelets, to which *Sauntress* would curtsey now and again, sending out a little rush of water as she slipped along. No lights, the Lizard and Eddystone were over our horizon and St Anthony's obscured by the land somewhere out ahead. No shore lights for these great headlands are deserted. No shipping, for we were far from the shipping lanes, just the glow of the compass light and that steady blessed breeze urging us on towards our destination.

Cradled in the bunk below, the motion was soothing almost beyond description, the trickle of the water along the planking, the gentle pressure as the boat lifted slightly, the stars through the open hatch. One almost wished it would not end."

It is strange, is it not, how we all seek something almost womb-like to soothe the soul. For some it is buried deep, overlaid by an excess of masculinity or practicality, but for others it lies scarcely beneath the surface, needing only the faintest prompting, to burst out, like some kind of flower.

"St Anthony's came clear, its great occulting light blinding us as it illuminated the sails and one by one the lights in Carrick Roads revealed themselves, confusing in their profusion. Harden up onto the wind, tack and lay St Mawes harbour, jump out of our skins as an unnoticed tug thunders by, hope to miss an unlit buoy, see it briefly in the gloom, feel our way in, further and further on a failing breeze until we can go on no more. It is well past midnight when the anchor rattles out and *Sauntress* lays at rest again after a long, long day.

And in the darkness, owls hooted."

We slept well that night, the incurable romantic and his solid, unimaginative, but faithful crew.

18

Across the Celtic Sea

MOUSEHOLE, THE HARBOUR DRIES. But outside, protected marginally by an islet, is an anchorage and here, rolling rhythmically, anchor chain grumbling on rock, *Sauntress* spent a rather restless night, for fair weather anchorage or no it was also a short cut for the Newlyn fishing craft, which, like fishing craft the world over, are in a hurry for the market and, you trust, keeping a good lookout as they thunder homewards, screaming gulls in pursuit.

Thus it was bleary-eyed that *Sauntress* crept clear on a misty morning, faint breaths from the hills, bound once again for those wilder shores. Crispin was crew, he whose shout "water at the mark" would fell an ox at one hundred yards, but otherwise mild-mannered and competent.

We had watered and provisioned at Falmouth, that lovely estuary, and were provided, as always, with the Admiralty pilot; charts; and all the odds and ends which would enable us to make repairs at sea: spare warps and halyards, toolbox, twine, needles and palm; wire cutters should, heaven help us, the mast go by the board; spare shackles, screws, nails; even sheets of ply to nail over any hole in the hull, for with the engineless sailing had come a determination to be self-reliant in all but the direst emergency.

The complete list of all that is squirrelled aboard *Sauntress* would make tedious reading, but would be familiar to the old kind of passage-maker: copper roves, little offcuts of leather, spare paraffin, spare lamp glasses, all the odds and ends which I could not bear to throw away, but one day, inevitably, would prove useful.

And always in the same place, like everything on the boat, instantly to hand, no need for lists, three anchors, the bower up forward, the fisherman on thirty fathoms of line stowed behind the mast, the kedge below on its short length of chain and line, the lead line to hand, the heaving line, a present from Crispin that, the binoculars, the best I could afford, the spare batteries for the radio and the not so useful, because very temperamental, GPS and the sextant and tables safely stowed below.

Midday found us becalmed once again off Land's End, waiting for a new wind. But there were new additions to the library aboard, for to add interest to the cruise I had brought along the accounts of those who had gone before us to south west Ireland: McMullen, in the mid-nineteenth century in his heavily-sparred *Orion* (and all his yachts were named after constellations), Claud Worth in 1889 in *Foam* and Commander Graham in the late 1930's in *Emanuel*; for it was their descriptions that had tempted us to follow, modestly, in their wake.

At last the wind filled in and when it came it was from the north-east, one of those anticyclones which, the barograph told us, was likely to last, a fair wind for Fastnet, and so it proved.

"Trade wind sailing must be like this," reads the log. Topsail drawing nicely, an empty sea, for there is virtually no shipping here, we reeled off the miles steadily, warm balmy days and bitterly cold nights, watch on watch as ever but, as always, checking, checking and checking again, for signs of chafe, anything amiss, any new and unfamiliar noise; lying on the deck, apparently idly, but in fact with eyes shaded, studying the rig.

And then I saw it. The boat would roll, the gaff swing, and as it swung an almost inaudible ping, like a harp string being plucked. Back on deck with the binoculars I studied the rig. Where was the sound coming from? Then I saw it. There is a bolt which holds the gaff jaws to the gaff, and on each roll, the bolt was catching on the throat halyard, and that was beginning to strand. We hove to on the port tack to consider the problem. For if left unattended to, the halyard would eventually part.

I went below for a small piece of leather, needle and palm. This we stitched around the halyard making a sleeve, and using the light line that normally keeps the heel of the topsail yard hard against the mast, when sailing with the topsail over double reefed main, sent this aloft until it protected the halyard against chafe and we could be on our way again. A note was made in the log to leather the bolt as a permanent solution and we could breathe easy again.

"Sunset like a molten bar," read the log. A colossal boom as someone, somewhere, broke the sound barrier and then, before you could write it, in rolled the fog. Well, we were out of the shipping lanes, about fifty miles by estimate from Fastnet, still with our north-easter, but as so often happens, an apparently empty sea by day becomes strangely populated by night. We could hear the throb of engines. A fishing boat or boats, most likely, erratic as always, sometimes louder, sometimes fainter, sometimes, momentarily a light, but always out there somewhere.

And so the night passed. But *Sauntress* was noiseless, slipping along with barely a murmur. We have no engine to drown out those warning sounds coming faintly through the gloom, sometimes bathed in a faint moon, sometimes clammily embracing, oil light in the cabin turned low to preserve night vision, eyes and ears as alert as they can be, we tiptoed onwards.

Dawn came with no change. We had run our distance. We hove to and pressed the dreaded GPS into service, marked the position on the chart, laid a new course and sailed on again. Repeated two or three times, for we were drawing ever closer to a strange landfall; we were about to stand off and heave to and wait for things to clear when whiteness at the foot of looming darkness told of cliffs.

Then a brief ray of sunshine and all cleared. And ahead lay the entrance to Baltimore harbour. Into which we slipped on a perfect Irish summer's day, green, sparkling and beautiful.

Distance run, about 200 nautical miles in forty-eight hours, including four hours becalmed off Land's End.

19

Roaring Water Bay

THERE ARE TWO WAYS OUT OF BALTIMORE HARBOUR, one easy, one difficult. Well, we had not come all this way for the easy life. What is more, "this passage is not recommended for yachts without auxiliary power"—and here speaks Nanny, in the form of a modern guide to south-west Ireland—is given the lie by none other than Commander Graham who in trenchant prose shows the thing in a rather different light. For he writes "it is a narrow intricate channel encumbered by shoals and rocky islets, but with the large scale Admiralty chart is not really difficult."

This of course was in *Emanuel*, a spitting image, near enough, of *Sauntress* and where *Emanuel* went we would follow. Mind you, we took it gently. The first stage, which Worth calls "a ditch," took us to Spanish Island in the entrance to the Ilen River. As remote a spot as you could wish for. Cows on the island had us speculating how they got there. Herons, seals, wildflowers, marshes, mosses, lichens, lush grass in little valleys and absolutely no "facilities" anywhere.

Here we anchored peacefully for the night. Replete from last night's meal ashore and clean, thanks to the Ile de Glenan showers. Thus our simple needs are satisfied.

Crispin went exploring and I studied the large scale Admiralty chart, memorizing each islet, each rock, each course, for there are no buoys here and once committed there would be no time either.

27 June 1999.
Forecast NW backing W or SW 3-4 or 5, occasionally 6, showers good.

With two reefs and foresail only we tacked our way through Mealbeg rock, the Catalogues Island, Two Women's Rock, an un-named Rock, Mullin's Rock, Toorane Rock, Calf island, Anima Rock, Sharragh's Rock, Carthy's Island, Amelia Rock, Castle Island and Bull Rock, all these had to be identified and cleared, and all in force 5 to 6 dead on the nose. 'On the margins', this passage, as the log notes, for there was no room for mistakes, the breakers on the shore sometimes perilously near, tide, wind, waves and spray all making pilotage just that bit more difficult. Nonetheless as we scurried between the reefs and islands, working our way to windward, there was time to admire the beauty of the scene, Bear Island and Fastnet Rock out to seaward, the mountains in the distance, the sun shining on all, it was salt-encrusted but triumphant that we brought up in the shelter of Schull harbour.

The meaning of all these names, or at least some of them, we were to discover later, for neither the Ilen River, nor Baltimore, nor yet Skibbereen, had finished with *Sauntress*.

Schull detained us hardly at all, and by next morning we were under way again, the delightfully Irish comment "the harbour-master has been dead these five years, so there will be no mooring charges" ringing in our ears, we scooted out in the general direction of Crookhaven only to find ourselves, not for the first time, nor the last, becalmed.

Well, there are places and places to be becalmed. Roaring Water Bay was as flat as a millpond. The evening was drawing in. Crookhaven beckoned 4 miles distant and fairly plainly nothing much was going to happen for many hours yet. We could have anchored, somewhere, in the lee of an island, but which would be the lee? And Roaring Water Bay as a name was surely no accident. Better not to dally unduly here.

Start the engine? But we do not have an engine, remember. But we do, the outboard, all 2 horsepower of Japanese efficiency. Tether the inflatable to *Sauntress*, install Crispin and the horses alongside and by nightfall this little procession was at the head of Crookhaven, a gulch sheltered behind the formidable Mizen Head, at anchor next to Granny Island. This concession to the modern world, if you want to call it that, gives us about a knot in calm water, enough, as has been seen to take us into harbour when the wind fails and enough, as will be seen later, to avoid more serious trouble.

20

Dunmanus Bay

29 June 1999.
Forecast W 3 – 4 backing S 4 – 5 occasionally 6.

"Y OU MUST VISIT DUNMANUS BAY. Everybody sails past and it is quite untouched."

Quite who the 'everybody' might be was a moot point. To date we had not seen a single yacht. But a remote spot in what was already a remote place was irresistible.

But my goodness it was bleak. Having cleared the immense Mizen Head, tides 4 knots, scooped up and bottled the purest virgin water for a God of Small Things, somewhere ashore, the Atlantic swells, such a feature of this coast, made themselves felt as we swept down the bay fifteen miles deep, with a rising following wind, past those forbidding headlands, with the surf bursting at their base, past Bird Island, scattering flocks of petrels as they bobbed on the water, the only sign of life in this desolate place, closing the southern shore, searching, searching for the elusive entrance to Dunmanus Harbour, our intended destination.

Closer and closer and still no obvious way in until suddenly there it was, a break in the rocks and the castle. We gybed at once and tore off on a reach for the entrance, racing in between the rock spits to find ourselves in a place of enchantment.

A little circular bay, a ruined castle and ancient arched stone bridge at the head. Two little beaches and above them a farmhouse peeping out from behind the trees. No yachts and a handful of fishing boats. We both walked ashore. The castle, its battlements broken in some siege, now housed only cows and ravens. The farm was for sale. The bridge led to a little inlet so one could row under its dripping arch, and the fisherman went off in the morning, seated in the stern, tiller under his arm and a seagull perched unconcerned on the prow. And the waves roared on the rocks outside.

Dangerously seductive these places. The castle, scarcely more than a tower, now the haunt of ravens, was the work of Donal More O'Mahony and not, as I thought at the time Donald O'Sullivan Beare, the last Gaelic chieftain of Ireland, whose ultimate redoubt, Dursey Island, beckoned in the morn.

Seductive, or was it something else? The first stirrings of recognition, roots, they call it, roots.

21

Through the Dursey Sound

30 June 1999.
W 3 – 4 backing SE 4 – 5 good becoming moderate.

DURSEY SOUND, A NARROW GULCH between the mainland and Dursey Island, saves about ten miles for a vessel bound from the south to the Kenmare River. The Admiral had things to say about this place, few of them all that encouraging, but the Admiral is seldom that. Prone to heavy squalls, strong tidal rips, a "dangerous rock in the middle onto which the N bound tide sets," confused seas set up by waves rebounding off the rocks, the threat of sudden wind shifts.

But if we did not try it we would always regret it and there would be no second chance.

Rounding Crow Head, having close-reached out of Dunmanus Bay, we came onto a run with the slightly unpleasant feeling that once committed there was no going back. Over-canvassed, nervous of a gybe, we dived into this witches' cauldron, hugging, for fear of that dangerous rock, the island shore, a biscuit's toss, Crispin's phrase, off the port beam, to be squirted out into the Kenmare River where, true to form, we received a violent squall, handed the topsail and tore off in suddenly atrocious visibility, up the Kenmare River, shores faintly visible in the gloom.

For a moment McMullen's words "the winds can blow with frightful force" on this coast came to mind, but bit by bit shelter was reached, we gybed around the reef which stretches half way across the Kenmare hereabouts and ran into the anchorage behind Garinish Island, at the foot of the little village of Sneem.

Perfect shelter and not, it need hardly be said, a yacht in sight.

And the Dursey Island we had passed a biscuit's toss away? Not quite the last redoubt, but a haven or so Donald O'Sullivan Beare believed, for when the test came, in the shape of vengeful Elizabethan troops, Dursey was the chosen sanctuary for the womenfolk and cattle, the Sound impassable, or so they believed.

But it was not.

And the shrieks were more than just the birds.

22

The Storm

2 July 1999.
S 5-7 occasionally 8, moderate to poor with fog patches.

DELIGHTFUL THOUGH THE ANCHORAGE WAS, it was hardly a place to leave *Sauntress*, for we had run out of time. Bearhaven in Bantry Bay seemed to promise at least a mooring, so to Bearhaven we were bound, forecast or no forecast.

We should perhaps have heeded McMullen and his "frightful force," for if ever there was a man who would never exaggerate, it was R.T. McMullen.

The log reads

"Well, we tried—full main became two reefs—jib and foresail became foresail only—*Sauntress* plunged wetly onwards, breasting big Atlantic swells—but each squall was worse than the one before—screaming in the rigging—and no land was to be seen. If it was like this in the lee of Dursey Island, how much worse outside—we never found out. The GPS, dizzy with our impossible motion, failed to get a fix so we ran—twice—once changing our mind to try again—but no, today was not to be—so here we lie and here we will stay."

And wisely so. *Sauntress* was as near to being overwhelmed as I have ever known her to be. Heaven knows what the wind force in the squalls was, but *Sauntress* could not stand up to them, we, the crew, were reduced to clinging on for dear life. To have pressed on would have been folly.

And this happy chance, for so it turned out to be, threw us into the arms of Tom and Pat, Seamus, Timmy and Mike, Mike O'Shea and an anchorage, the like of which I defy you to find anywhere in this wide world.

Welcome to Ireland, the land of my forebears.

23

Garinish and The Secret Garden

"**T**IS A MOORING YOU WILL BE WANTING,**" said Tom.

Tom was one of those people, and fortunately they still exist, to whom generosity and grace came natural. True, his comment "nobody does that now" as we brought up under sail was followed by "Oh, real sailors" as we explained we had no choice. And true, too, that the question of what the mooring might cost, and who would lay it, required more than one evening over a Guinness to negotiate; but the ensuing generosity, Sunday lunches cooked by that paragon of the Irish hearth, Pat Downey, home-made biscuits and home-made cake, lettuce and eggs on the deck in the morning, all these and more told their own story.

For Tom and Pat were humble folk, in the very best sense of the word, the kind to whom it would be unthinkable to turn away the stranger at the door; Tom, with his easy smile and gentle self-deprecating humour, his assortment of jobs: grave digger for Sneem, gardener, small-holder; steady, thoughtful— it was clear that *Sauntress* would be at home here. So she stayed.

As moorings go, it was without equal.

The shelter was complete. There were, as ever, no other yachts. The wild-life had Georgie, who soon came visiting, in raptures. The evenings echoed to the sound of the creak, splash, creak, splash, of the Sneem Sein boat or the cry of a smallholder, searching, searching for a lost cow. And those evenings lingered, in that way they have in high summer in the far west of Ireland, prac-tically until midnight.

And Garinish, the Kenmare Garinish had history enough. Once this place had been a kind of plaything to Lord Dunraven, one of those Anglo-Irish landlords, and his whim, apart from challenging twice for the America's cup in two successive *Valkyries*, had been to lay out Garinish as a sub-tropical garden, his other yacht, *Cariad*, you can see her just, lying on a mooring off the bight.

Although his Lordship was long gone another absentee had come, bought the island, and it had fallen to Tom, Seamus, Timmy and Mike, to set about restoring the place to its former glory, four full-time gardeners, no less.

Seamus of the four was the studious one. Off to Dublin for photographs from the Lawrence collection, Garinish in its heyday. Delving into the archives, he unearthed his Lordship's layout for the garden, over which together we pored after one particularly violent storm, in the boathouse that lay at the head of the bight. We became involved.

And we became lazy.

Resting slightly on our laurels, I surveyed the harbour, lead line from dinghy, wandered, with permission, in those gardens, picked herbs, dug peat and with only the slightest prompting from Tom uncovered my own Irish roots.

And in that survey, checking the depths, especially how close we could stand in to the rocks which fringed the bight, we were in good company. For here is McMullen in *Orion* in August 1869, in the very same spot

"10 P.M. anchored in Garinish Bay, which in its safest and most protected part is so confined by a dangerous reef, that I went ahead in the boat and examined that side of the anchorage by rowing from Garinish Island to the reef, from the reef to the mainland at a right angle, and then diagonally to the spot where the anchor was to be let go."

Oh yes it was narrow, but safe.

Regatta day came. I was put on rather ineffectual point duty. It rained in that Irish way. It was an occasion worthy of Somerville and Ross. For next to horses, the fearsomely fought Sein boat regatta was old Ireland come to life. The weather-beaten faces, the sodden shoes, the "testing, testing," the "we'll be waiting just that bit, O'Flaherty is on his way" (broken down somewhere). The roars of encouragement, when finally proceedings got under way; the red faces, for the Guinness flowed freely; the crabs caught;

Tom in the workboat, thundering in pursuit, for the thing was best seen from the water; Sneem rather satisfactorily winning, *The Liberator* ("after Daniel O'Connell, of course," with just a touch of surely you should know that, being Irish and all) came second.

It lacked only Lady Dunraven to award the prizes.

But this, you will object, is not sailing.

And you would be right. But first here is Georgie, the faithful Georgie, filling our usually strictly nautical log with his raptures, for south west Ireland is a naturalists' paradise

"30 April 2000. Awoke late and ate hearty breakfast. At least three pairs of herons nesting in the tops of trees on west side of inlet. Very busy feeding noisy young. Black guillemots thrilled us and our cameras. Hobby flew over briefly. Then came a great northern diver, very rare and beautiful, feeding within 50 metres of *Sauntress*. Hooded crows abundant. In the afternoon we went for a row between Garinish and the mainland through that lovely straight channel, were observed quietly but closely by seals and on return were surprised by the number of fish jumping.

2 May 2000. Tom, Seamus, Timmy and Mike all back at work today. Nicola and I went to the island at 1430 and spent all that time amazed by an Irish garden in early May. With Seamus' say so we picked fennel, sorrel, parsley, chard and mint for boiled spuds. Excellent supper. Mike O'Shea came 1100 to install new switch panel. Then hoisted me up the mast to check the masthead lights. All working well. Finished with the compass light.

3 May 2000. Cloudless day. Spent day out fishing and on island. Martin, you must get to see the island in May. Superb."

24

Valentia Island and The Skelligs

Garinish to Valentia. 19.06.2000. S3-4 occasionally 5. Barograph 1010.
Crew George.

THIS WAS TO BE A SUMMER CRUISE, up north as far as conditions permitted. At virtually the solstice we would have light until midnight, being 10° west, a consideration on this coast which is very poorly lit and buoyed hardly at all.

And whether you choose to be guided by McMullen or the Admiralty pilot, the verdict is the same: "when the coast is densely shrouded in mist, navigation is extremely dangerous."

So it was with a degree of trepidation we interrupted the Garinish idyll, hoisted all sail, topsail included, cast off in the bight and waited to see what would happen. The answer, for a moment, was nothing, then a puff came, *Sauntress* pivoted on her heel and away, bound for Valentia, we went.

"0745 wind light and variable, visibility moderate."

"0900 wind S2-3, course 240, visibility poor, Illaunegh Island bears 00 degrees, 0.5 m."

"0945 wind S4, course 240, visibility poor, log 1.85, topsail off."

"1210 wind S3, course 327, visibility poor, log 11.08 Rounded Scarriff Island, course change for Bolus head."

All marks disappeared in the murk. We ran on blind on a compass course, trusting to clear both Bolus Head and the off-lying Lemon Rock, then Puffin Island and finally Bray Head, the westernmost point of Valentia Island; but we had one trick up our sleeve, the brand new GPS. This gave us a position, on our course, but much further on than the patent log would have us believe, the reason, plainly, being a fierce north-running tide. Reassured, we stowed the thing and in due course up came Bray Head, around which we gybed, expecting shelter from the hills.

We should, given our experience of Dursey, have known better, for instead of shelter came squalls, a smart reduction of sail and, as the wind continued to freshen, the entrance to Valentia harbour opened up. It is between two rock spits, half a cable wide, and is entered on leading marks. The wind, now about force 6, was blowing straight out. However *Sauntress* proved equal to the challenge, short tacking smartly in the narrow entrance, and once in anchored in 15 foot in Glanleam Bay, under Glanleam House, another of those Irish subtropical gardens.

"Wind S5 log 28.2, anchored Valentia harbour after an exciting tack in." It was, in short, a satisfactory end to a satisfactory passage, 34 nautical miles across the ground, the difference of 6 being made by the strong north flowing tide.

Oh the best laid plans of mice and men.

Our anchorage seemed secure so we went ashore in search of this and that, specifically paint brushes, as *Sauntress* needed a scrub and antifoul, an expedition which involved a ferry, a four mile walk and plenty of Irish rain, to be greeted on our return, by the alarming sight of *Sauntress* damn near on the rocks.

Naturally enough we immediately cleared out, with difficulty, for when the anchor came up, so did a vast amount of kelp, the bane of this anchorage, as we had just learned, and tacked down to a very uncomfortable mooring off Knightstown.

The log takes up the story:

"21.06.2000. Longest day and the first day of summer. Here, marooned in Valentia, with SW5-7, rain showers and a good fire." So much for choosing mid-summer for our cruise. And here we were destined to stay. The entrance, as the Admiralty pilot wrote, a mass of breakers in the strong NW wind, seas bursting on the rocks, spray carried streaming down wind. We moved to the Portmagee channel, where we anchored peacefully and safely, slipped at a local yard, were scrubbed, antifouled and, nominally, surveyed and waited for a break.

Needless to say Worth had been here before us. He was, like McMullen, patriotic in that Victorian way.

"Friday May 24th 1889. We left Kilmakilloge under all sail with ensign at the peak in honour of the Queen's birthday, sailed close past Bolus Head and Puffin Island and entered the western end of the sound which divides Valentia Island from the mainland. Off Knights Town we anchored in 3 fathoms. Whilst we were stowing the canvass, a gentleman came off in a boat and invited us to dine with him."

Infuriatingly, Worth leaves it at that, but 'gentleman' in his vocabulary has a pretty narrow meaning. He anchored in full view of Glanleam House, as did we, and Glanleam was the home to the Knights of Kerry, enlightened Irish landlords, and that ostentatious ensign, flown in honour of the Queen's birthday, could hardly have gone unnoticed.

1889 is too late for the nineteenth Knight, an obviously congenial character, fully deserving the epithet enlightened, "whose hospitality at Glanleam was enjoyed by the Prince of Wales and other distinguished guests," so again, and as with that other sub-tropical garden, we are left with fleeting glimpses of a vanished world, or as Worth calls it, in an uncharacteristic flush of romanticism, fairyland.

But it is true in a way. Worth, McMullen, Lord and I suppose it has to be Lord Dunraven, and the yachts they sailed, *Foam*, *Tern III*, *Cariad*, *Valkyrie*, *Orion*, flit dimly almost fairy-like through the Irish mists, seduced each and every one of them, as we were being seduced, by that intangible something that is the south-west coast of Ireland.

The only light note in this sadly aborted cruise came when the yard owner, one Pat Curtin, clearly expecting a foul-up, having stood goggle-eyed on the hard, muttering "where is the engine," rubbed his hands and remarked "now we shall see the master at work." But backed foresail and spring from the stern took us nicely clear to hoist the main and run back down to our anchorage, having, as my old mentor Kenneth would have said, satisfactorily wiped their eyes. For it is a point of honour, smartly to handle your ship.

It remained only to sail, in fact, drift home again, via, by George's special request, the Skelligs. For here, as Georgie knew, we could see European storm petrels, northern divers, gannets, fulmars, Manx shearwaters, black legged kittiwakes, common guillemots, razorbills and Atlantic puffins.

For once the visibility was good. Progress however was painfully slow. The sea was slumbering, but breathing deeply, that oily Atlantic swell. We were, as always, the only yacht, indeed the only vessel at sea, lazy, slow and slightly frustrating progress. The Skelligs, those lonely sentinels, were a kind of mirage, close enough now to see the birds swirling and screaming. The log has a photograph, reading Great Skellig, Little Skellig, Lemon Rock, transit. They could not have been more than a mile away. But time was running out. If we turned now and ran in for the land, at three knots we would take five hours to reach the anchorage again, and in five hours it would be dark. And the Kenmare is unlit, the night would be moonless, so reluctantly up went the helm, we set the tow foresail and big jib and crept up to a respectable three knots or so, bound once again for home.

Five hours at three knots. The Skelligs lay astern now, as the sun lowered. But to the south, maybe ten miles distant, off Dursey Head lay The Cow and The Bull. There was time to open McMullen again. "The wind light from the SSW and a swell from the west it was late afternoon when we came up with the Cow." He heaves to, launches the boat and rows through the great cavern of the Bull, having been momentarily becalmed in the lee of the Cow, sounding as he went, and then turns.

"Fine as the entrance looked on the NE side, it was not to be compared to the grandeur of the SW, upon which the sun shone, lighting up huge blocks, and giving it the appearance of an immense castle gateway, swarmed to the top with thousands of gannets... the scene was altogether so lively and enchanting that I was delighted and turned the boat's head with great reluctance to pass through the cavern again to the *Orion*, which at that moment, happened to be in line with the centre of the arch, about half a mile off, looking, with the sun upon her, like a framed picture."

That was written 140 years ago. But out here, nothing had changed, the same wild and haunting coast, the same treacherous weather, capable at times of frightening us out of our wits, but at others as now, casting that extraordinary spell, the same lack of lights and beacons, and in a sense the same sensations. The same limitations and even, dare I say it, the same type of sailing.

There was one final log entry. "Drift in on the last of the breeze in fading light, good end to a long day." And although we did not know it then, the yacht that had taken our mooring had been watching, as in the last of the light, this apparition from another age stole silently across glassy water, all sail set, to anchor at last.

So ended our summer cruise.

25

The Luck Penny

THE MOORING, SO ROMANTIC IN SUMMER, was a different proposition in winter. Sheltered from all quarters it might be, but sheltered in
the west of Ireland is a relative term, for the storms that batter that coast have
to be seen to be believed.

And a stupid oversight nearly lost me the boat, for I had failed to take one
elementary precaution, which was to parcel the mooring line against chafe.
And so, one night it parted, *Sauntress* was driven ashore, and by rights that
should have been the end of the story, being as how there are rocks and reefs
everywhere.

But no, the weary cherub stretched a hand once more, and guided the er-
rant *Sauntress* into the one reed bed in the place. And not only that, Tom,
Seamus, Timmy, Mike and the skipper of the Sherky Star, the fishing boat
that shared the bight, hesitated not a second. Two nights' work in appalling
conditions had her back, undamaged, on her mooring, before even I could
reach her.

And never even a whisper of salvage.

"It could happen," they said generously, "to any of us."

Nonetheless the idyll was drawing to a close.

For three years *Sauntress* had lain behind Garinish Island. Friendships had
been made. And however much the place was home, it was time to move on
again. So for the last time, Georgie as crew again, we slipped the mooring.
A bitter-sweet moment, for I knew we would never come back. One cannot.
And it would have been wrong to have tried. Letters were exchanged for a
while and then silence. What became of Tom and Pat, the absentee landlord,

the garden they worked so hard to restore, I shall never know. And nor do I think I want to.

It is better, as Tom said, to remember the good times and leave it at that.

For once, a gentle breeze blew, the skies were clear, Dursey, Bantry, Dunmanus, Mizen Head, in all their grandeur passed in our lee, and on a rising tide we ran up the Ilen River, unmarked needless to say, to bring up, head to wind at Hegarty's Boatyard, Old Court, Skibbereen, proprietor Liam Hegarty, the card printed in green.

The last wooden boatyard in Ireland.

These places, so visually unappealing, hide treasures and Hegarty's Boatyard was no exception. These treasures come in two forms, the bits and pieces a wooden boat always needs but are now so hard to find, and treasures of the other kind, people.

If you want to be rich, do not run a boatyard, still less a wooden boatyard. But, if you want to put your finger on the pulse of a place, learn, somewhat in awe, deep and arcane things, then you could do a lot worse than spend time here. The shyly smiling never-to-be-found Liam hoisted *Sauntress* ashore, propped her up on oil drums and returned to whatever problem was bugging him that day.

John, the partner in the business, soon made us feel welcome. "You will be cold." He arrived with a heater. "You will want some music." He arrived with a wireless. "You might be interested in this." He arrived with a book, *The Lobster Boats of Heir Island and Roaring Water Bay* (Cormac Levis 2002).

Suddenly a new voice was added to our little library. And it was an Irish voice. For whilst the likes of Sir Richard Sutton's *Genesta* was winning the 1,000 guinea Jubilee Race "around her Majesty's home dominions" (1897), Worth was commenting "what surprised us was that though these waters appear to be swarming with fish, very few Irishmen take the trouble to catch them" (1899), and R.T. McMullen was admiring a "good view of the real Irish 'holdings'" (1897 again). Cormac Levis throws, perhaps not surprisingly, a rather different light on these Victorian high jinks.

Neither Tom, nor Pat, nor Liam, nor John ever breathed a word about Irish history, neither the potato famine of 1847, nor the Civil War, nor any other of the myriad things on which one might think they were perfectly entitled to hold forth. Cormac Levis' book thus served a dual purpose, to explain just why, once again, the Lobster Boats were being built, not for fishing, but for a new and prosperous customer, keeping, as they say the old crafts alive.

And to give the lie to Worth's rather thoughtless comment, "very few Irishmen take the trouble to catch them." Cormac Levis quotes from the *Royal Commission on Irish Oyster Fisheries* (1870) "so broken down (by the potato famine) were the thousands of fishermen that they were physically incapable of putting to sea. Multitudes had to part with their boats and gear for anything that they could to procure the means of appeasing the hunger of themselves and their families."

But then, once on a rain and windswept road, the very picture of desolation, an anonymous stranger poured forth all the others never said.

The adze flew, scattering oak chips.

A rhythmic thump, thump, thump, long into the evening told of caulking seams. New timbers were steamed into position, fastened with trunnels, lines were taken off the half derelict *Hanorah*, not quite the last surviving lobster boat, and Nigel Towse, responsible for this resurrection, looked at the tangle that was *Sauntress*' rigging and remarked, "I love unravelling a mess like that."

Nigel, another incomer, steered the skipper away from the expensive tourist-orientated bars and terraces of Baltimore, to an eatery in Skibereen, utilitarian, very much roast and three veg with sticky pudding, custard and copious cups of tea. He had wandered in from some town in the English midlands and never left, found the *Hanorah*, begged a corner in the yard and started restoring.

In this atmosphere of proper ship-wrighting, faithful recreation of a half lost past, *Sauntress* was very much at home. It hardly mattered that Worth's insensitive comment was curiously wide of the mark, one had only to read

Cormac Levis to see that. What mattered was that he had rescued the history in the same way as Nigel Towse was rescuing *Hanorah*.

Cormac Levis' book has a touching dedication:

For Saoirse
13 August – 19 October 1998

With which Irish history elbows its way in again. For *Saoirse* was also the name of the yacht, built here in Baltimore, to his own design, by Conor O'Brien, "a haughty little Irishman, whose attitude to the English was patronising at best" (*The Circumnavigators*, Don Holm), *Saoirse* meaning freedom in Gaelic. Which was no accident, for O'Brien was the first man, so Don Holm asserts, never mind Irishman, to voyage around the world in a yacht south of the three stormy capes, flying the flag of the Irish Free State.

Haughty or not, he consented, or so one must assume, to the introduction to his account of the voyage, being written by none other than that quintessential Englishman, Claud Worth, who keeps popping up in these pages, not only because we kept crossing his wake, but because no biography of this man exists, and who, for all his high Victorian attitudes, occasionally allows a glimpse of the more intimate kind, as in this little gem:

"It has become the custom of the ship that the crew do not turn out until the skipper has given them an early cup of tea."

A practice, I might add, which prevails aboard *Sauntress*.

Born in 1869, so he was a mere 20 years old when he and his chum Green took *Foam* to South West Ireland, Claud Worth was a successful ophthalmic surgeon. He is described in his obituary (he died on June 24 1934) as quiet and unassuming in manner and very successful in handling small children. Indeed it is a kindly steady gaze that he returns to the photographer, with more than a trace of a twinkle in his eye. Patriotic to a fault, for when caught in L'Abervrac'h in August 1914, on the outbreak of the Great War he writes:

"The one question seemed to be 'Will England join?' I replied that England would certainly carry out her engagements. 'But Monsieur, suppose there is only a verbal promise of support, no written agreement, you under-

stand?' I answered somewhat brusquely that Britain's word was as good as her bond."

Then, as he lays up *Tern III* for the duration comes this positively quixotic passage, inspired clearly by Erskine Childers and that other book *The Riddle of the Sands*:

"In the Wash and elsewhere I have been accustomed to get about among sands in thick weather and late one autumn spent six weeks in exploring the German North Sea Coast. In Portsmouth there are plenty of torpedo boats which are too small for ordinary North Sea work. I had a plan, but the authorities would have none of it."

Curious how these lives intertwine, Claud Worth, R.T. McMullen, Erskine Childers, Conor O'Brien, Commander Graham; but then a sudden gust had the lamp flicker. Enough of this reverie, for the moment anyway, it said, for spring was late this year, gale after gale roared and hustled, the boat shaking, loose things clattering, reeds bending and we worked steadily on.

The time came to pay.

Liam, looking a little embarrassed, muttered something about paperwork. "What's wrong with cash Liam?" He punched a few keys on the calculator, the only piece of technology to be seen, showed me the result and wondered if I could manage by lunchtime, it being Friday and he having the lads' wages to pay. The notes were counted all correct, and with a shy smile Liam peeled off the top one and gave it back.

"That's for luck," the Luck Penny.

A discreet tap on the coach-roof.

"You will be joining us for the festival?"

Tousled hair, youthful face glowing with enthusiasm, how could we resist? But father Neptune said otherwise, and with a last vicious snap of the fingers sank a Galway Hooker on the way, for all that Liam, Nigel and the owner dropped all and raced to the rescue; it was too late, she had dragged, and that, sad to say, was that.

"No lives were lost and that is a blessing" can have been scant consolation to the owner. Superfluous perhaps to comment that just as at Garinish, the first and only thought was to help. These people live too close to the sea and its moods to think otherwise.

At last the skies cleared.

"You racing tomorrow? We want to see how she goes."

Every Sunday lunch-time and every Wednesday evening in the summer there would be racing in Baltimore Harbour. Liam would be there in *Fion*, so would Nigel in his now completed replica of the *Hanorah*. And plenty others too.

"When is the start Liam?"

"When the last boat arrives."

Shades of Somerville and Ross.

But we were not much better, a frantic last moment rush, George up the mast, provisions forgotten (solved by Ted), the boat in an uncharacteristic mess, we were towed down the Ilen and deposited in the melee that was allegedly the start.

After pretending we were too grown up for this kind of thing, the old bug quickly bit. George, who as is known thinks little of this kind of lark, doing his reluctant bit, *Sauntress* zipped round the not very demanding course, won her class and by morning was gone.

Not, however, before a little prize-giving by the pub on Sherkin Island, Liam and family presiding; some shy and regretful goodbyes, not only to Liam and the others but to the Ireland that had by turns entranced and scared us, for by tomorrow evening all land would have faded from sight.

26

Becalmed

To THE ETERNAL QUESTION "what do you do when there is no wind?," there is but one answer, "wait." A better question might be "what is it like to be becalmed?"

And to that I can certainly give an answer.

If you are in the way of shipping, you are in for an anxious time. If you are close to a reef, and the tide is setting you towards it, you tow the boat clear. And that was what happened on the passage from Baltimore to Plymouth. The wind failed us as we were clearing the Seven Stones, onto which, unless we did something, we would be set. So we launched the dinghy and towed *Sauntress* clear.

And once clear, yes, we waited.

Gradually the swell left behind by the now absent wind subsided until at last all was completely still. We were several miles from Land's End and a fair distance from the Scilly Islands. Not only was the sea like polished glass. There was not a sound. Not even a creak of the rig.

This has a curious effect on the mind, mine anyway. For since the world is holding its breath, almost literally, you begin to talk in whispers. Your movements become slow and deliberate so as not to disturb the unwonted peace, the type probably only known to moun-taineers where there is a total absence of any sign whatsoever of human activity.

And the longer the silence and motionlessness last, the more the sensa-tion is heightened. In this case we waited from dawn to almost dusk, which in summer is nigh on eighteen hours. Joseph Conrad in *The Shadow Line* explores the effect of a prolonged calm on the mariner's mind, and although he denies there is any supernatural element, there is a curious sense of menace in so much unnatural stillness. A strange sense of foreboding as though in the very act of sleeping nature is reminding you of her terrible power.

The modern sailor, who has merely to start the engine, will know nothing of this. And the loss is all his.

For as we lay still, the log line plumbing the depths, set, as we could see, by the tide first this way then that, with something Conrad calls stealthy power, the sea came alive. And with Georgie aboard it was like having your very own David Attenborough. Porpoises gambolled for our especial benefit. The surface breaks, a turtle's head, a great monster paddles lazily by; a Loggerhead Turtle, Georgie opines. A sea serpent of some kind wriggled on the surface. Diving birds feast on pilchards.

The sun sinks.

Still no wind.

Supper comes and is cleared away again. Soon the tide will turn and take us…

And then, almost when you are least expecting it, comes that unmistakable line on the horizon, the darkening of the surface which indicates wind, a new wind. Still the boat lies motionless, still waiting, but then a breath. You feel it on your cheek first, then a faint whisper in the ear, the familiar sound of a gentle caressing breeze. It is the sound you will hear if you stand on the foredeck of your ship, at anchor in some creek, a faint land breeze over the marshes.

And here out at sea you hear it again, just as still, just as peaceful, the soft voice of the wind speaking, promising. The long wait is over and you know it is over. This is not some fickle breath to tease and die again. This is the real thing. The dark line tells you that.

Tiny ripples on the surface and the mainsail hanging limp all those hours stirs a little. Silently still, the ship begins to slip through the water, log line straightening, feeling for the new wind and then comes a slight heeling, the first chatter of the water under the bow.

The helmsman steers with more confidence now. The speed picks up more, the chatter becomes a steady murmur, the sails swell once again. The wind hums, the boat is alive again, racing across a still sleeping sea, the long hours of waiting now just a memory.

And that feeling of a new beginning, that awakening, is more powerful in its way than any experience at sea you can name.

27

Two Days with Jenny

(An interlude)

To bring up smartly all standing at the head of the Tamar, on a sluicing tide and hemmed in by moored yachts, was as nice a piece of boat handling as you could wish for, and one of which I was justifiably proud.

Even the world weary dock hand was impressed.

But pride, as ever, cometh before a fall.

"Unfit for passage making," read the surveyors report. Oh dear, that Irish rain.

Poor *Sauntress* was carted off on a lorry for Toosey and the skilled attention of Andrew Balfe, known to all as Droid. And her skipper was left bereft, wandering disconsolately somewhere in the fens like a junkie without a fix until…

He saw a sign, "Boats."

And down a track, there, sure enough were boats, Broads boats, wooden Broads boats at that, and these boats were for hire. The long hot summer was still hanging on, shirtsleeves and sunbathing in late September, blue skies, a warm caressing breeze, and for most, holidays long over. The scene, the water, the reeds, the wide open skies, the boats waiting, was impossibly inviting. A notion formed, and no sooner formed blossomed into an idea.

Jenny, bless her, was well past her prime, but that was precisely her charm. She had an engine, a Stuart Turner, but she had something else. A quant, a wooden pole maybe twelve foot long, one end with a fork, like misshapen gaff jaws, and the other with a rounded knob, fitting comfortably into the hand, with a feel which only wood can give, when old and worn smooth by constant use. This and the sails were to be her means of propulsion.

"You won't be wanting to pass under Potter Heigham Bridge?" this said more as a statement than a question, so that left Hickling Broad, Horsey Mere and assorted dykes to be explored, enough surely, especially for the novice to Broads sailing.

It had taken a bit of persuading to induce them to allow a single hander to hire her—"she has a jib you know"—so to slightly doubtful looks, *Jenny* was warped into position to cast off and tack, it had to be tack, against wind and tide, another surprise, the short stretch to Candle Dyke. The jib set appallingly, the main no better, and *Jenny* sidled as much as sailed, tack by laborious tack towards her first objective. To port lay reed beds, and to starboard a kind of quay where impassive men sat, fishing rods extending annoyingly far out, for which *Jenny*, it was plain, would have to give way.

A helpful sign informed us that ahead lay Martham Broad and to port Hickling Broad so, sheets eased, *Jenny* lifted her skirts and ran off downwind and into the unknown. All around were reeds rustling and bending to the breeze. "Keep to the right," read the signs, "keep to the right." A strange world this. No navigation at night, no compass, no depth sounder, no "port to port," no view, for the reeds were too tall for this, but power gave way to sail. That much at least was familiar.

Horsey Mere beckoned for no better reason than it seemed somewhere to go, and would involve a small challenge, the passage down Meadow Dyke, no wider than a trout stream and, like any self-respecting trout stream, with banks adorned with bushes. For a while close on the wind, *Jenny* slipped along, but then came a bend, a bungled tack, and the satisfying spectacle, for the inevitable onlookers, of *Jenny* drifting ignominiously stern first into the reeds.

Time for the quant...

Now the reason for the raised eyebrows at single handing became clear. The quant needed two hands, the sheets another and the tiller yet another, and the quant, as it sank deep into the mud, was all too ready to play a game, "see if I can't pull you overboard," "see if I can't pull you overboard."

A sharp little twist at the end of the push put paid to that little trick, but as for walking nonchalantly down the side deck, leaning on the quant as one went, forget it. More of the same found us at last on a decent expanse of water, Horsey Mere.

Here, with evening drawing in, shades of purple, the reeds as far as the eye could see, and not a person or a boat in sight, *Jenny* anchored. Anchoring involved lifting a large rectangular iron weight on the fore-deck, attached to a length of doubtful line and dropping the thing overboard. *Jenny* brought up and was at rest. Her defects could wait until morning. The galley was in the cockpit. Lift a lid and there was a stove. New potatoes bubbled away. Minted lamb cutlets from the butchers in Martham sizzled, a whisky lay to hand and all seemed right with the world.

Perfick in fact.

The same could be said of the dawn. A slight mist hung over still water. Stately rows of ducks swam to wherever ducks swim and the sun slowly rose. If the lamb cutlets were good the bacon was out of this world. Home smoked Norfolk bacon from that butcher in Martham, and new laid eggs too.

Poor *Jenny*, she deserved some attention. An hour or so had the gaff saddle greased (with butter), the head of the jib re-secured to the eyelet, the lacing at the luff of the main reset, the lacing on the gaff and the boom attended to, the standing rigging set up again and the pennant at the masthead flying as it should, not upside down in the rigging. *Jenny* responded to this treatment by tacking around in Horsey mere looking in vain for the northern passage out. Bored with this fruitless activity, she shouldered her way back down Meadow Dyke, bouncing off one bank or the other, generally getting in the way to emerge once more in Heigham Sound, an impossibly grand name for a patch of shallow water.

Now the breeze blew and she shot off, metaphorically speaking, up Hickling Broad to a sound all too like running aground on shingle. This was a puzzle. Enormous stakes lined the navigable area, suitably painted red or green, and tempting though it was, *Jenny* had not broken the rules and strayed. Lift the lid on the dreaded Stuart Turner lurking in its box and there was the answer. A revolving propeller shaft, probably in need of lubrication.

This was a good breeze and as a result we soon ran out of broad. Tacking back was fun but ultimately futile. We would have to find something else to do. Downwind lay some navigation marks, red and green buoys, and a sort of hole in the bushes into which a boat disappeared. Irresistible. *Jenny* followed, and as she followed, a new danger to navigation presented itself.

Trees.

This impossibly narrow ditch, called Catfield Dyke, was overhung by branches just waiting to get entangled with some inaccessible part of the rig. So to showers of leaves and the cracking of twigs *Jenny* half sailed, half drifted her way the better part of a mile to a rather strange quay, where a single taciturn fisherman confirmed that yes, this was the end of navigation, probably blaming *Jenny*'s silent intrusion for a poor catch today.

Getting out again, *Jenny* showed her mettle, her tendency to go sideways when on the wind countered by judicious application of the quant, to the appreciation of a picnicking party, who passed a beer as we quanted by. A tacking match with a dinghy (*Jenny* lost) brought us back pretty much to the yard, but not before *Jenny* had caused alarm aboard the oddly named *Wot No Paint*, by attempting to smite her (unpainted) topsides on a tack.

Jenny tacked in her own particular way. Rather deliberately, surprisingly surely, but with a tendency to swing her stern around and hit the reeds, or whatever happened to be in the way, in this case *Wot No Paint*. (The malicious would say there was none left over to judge by the make-up on that outraged face).

Turning left, (for you could hardly call it port), *Jenny*, rounded off her day by a smart sail, off the wind for once, down the river Thurne. Here, to begin with the banks were lined by summer chalets, one with a little row of chairs on the veranda, painted, the first one with the word hip, and the next, with the word hip, and the last? Hooray.

The jib, which set like a sack and pulled the bow off the wind horribly, had been dispensed with, but as we came on the wind at a bend in the river, further humiliation, needless to say to an audience, as *Jenny* sulked, paid off and became totally unmanageable. Wandering nonchalantly up to the fore-deck to drop the mud weight fooled only the skipper.

Under the coamings were two, in effect, half fisherman's anchors, one fluke only. Purpose? Attach to a line, throw well into the reeds and you were moored. Thus *Jenny* passed her second night. The forecast said the weather would break tomorrow. Up at dawn, not a breath of wind. Yes, there was the Stuart Turner, but there was also the quant.

So quant it was.

Sometimes *Jenny* would think about sailing, but not for long and drift sideways. A steady rhythm, drop the quant and find the bottom. Soft mud? Do not lean too hard. Shingly? You can give a good shove. Get bored. Drop the weight on the fore-deck and rest. The first time that happened in the stillness of the dawn, it was like firing a gun. Wave upon wave of angrily protesting wildfowl took to the air. Truly this was an extraordinary place, with its keep to the right, neither sea nor land, the bizarre names and the oddly taciturn encounters, the sailing which is not really sailing, and that miraculous butcher.

Then the wind came. And later the rain. But by then *Jenny* was back in the hands of the yard and her skipper staring over the grey wastes from a hotel window in Aldeburgh.

A square-rigger butted her way south, under engine.

Summer was gone.

28

Sauce for the Goose is . . .

THE GOOSE, IT NEED HARDLY BE SAID, is any one of Claud Worth's yachts, from *Tern* at 6½ tons to *Tern IV* at a whopping 40 or so tons and the gander is none other than the diminutive *Sauntress*.

The sauce is the squaresail.

As a fine shipwright once remarked, if you have a vintage gaff cutter yacht, Claud Worth is the reference book for you and that is as true of the squaresail as anything else.

Here he is in 1895 on the first *Tern* off Scotland:

"The squaresail had kept the vessel steady, but we found running under fore and aft canvass a very different matter"—Claud Worth, *Yacht Cruising*, p92.4th edition, J.D. Potter 1934

That extract alone is enough to grab your attention, for a gaffer on a run in a blow is a handful, griping, threatening to gybe, fighting you all the way, yet the squaresail, it would appear, is a different matter. Interest quickened, you read on.

"A squaresail in a small vessel requires scarcely any gear, gybing entails no extra work, it can be carried in any weather in which it is safe to run before the wind at all."

And again,

"A lifting sail, not a pressing sail;" "it should be made of light material a little heavier than a spinnaker;" "the sail is set flying with three halyards;" "I have seen the sail got down quite easily by one man in a strong wind." "It should have a deep reef or bonnet." More in the same vein may be found in *Yacht Cruising*, pages 370 to 373.

Look elsewhere and it is the same story. Here, for instance is William Albert Robinson, writing in *Deep Water and Shoal*: "At all times it pulled harder and steadier than any other sail on board ... not to mention greatly increasing the ease of steering and ease of mind too."

Turn to Conor O'Brien and there it is again. In fact read carefully the classics of the inter-war years and time and time again the references come. And they are joyful references. They loved the sail. They revelled in its power. So what in the name of something had happened?

It was time to find out.

The only problem was it had disappeared. Nobody knew how to make a squaresail for a yacht. Enquiries brought an incredulous blank from sailmakers, fearful perhaps for their reputation.

But as with the discarding of auxiliary power, if I did not try I would always regret it, so to hell with convention, spinnakers, twins and the rest of it. The obsession was too deep.

It took time, years in fact, but in the end we got there. For not only had the thing to be designed, made, rigged, played with, but we had to find a sailmaker who was prepared to take the proposition seriously, one who understood the "deep reef or bonnet," who sympathised, who did not think the skipper mad. But I was prepared to wait, fatalistically, for that moment which one day I knew would come.

Worth had the advantage of us. His lament "I will never again go to sea without a squaresail" was because his yacht, *Tern IV*, was new. He was uncertain what area of sail the ship would bear, but once his mind was made up he would go back to Ratsey and Lapthorn and order it, deep reef or bonnet and all. Perhaps in their archives the patterns are still there. Perhaps had I asked, they would have rootled around and risen to the challenge? It would be interesting to know. Instead I waited, fatalistically, as one waits for a wind, a fair tide, a slant, an inspiration, a chance encounter, for one is almost with that "Allah will provide" which so fascinated Allan Villiers in his intriguing *Sons of Sinbad*, an attitude of mind which precisely suited *Sauntress* and her skipper. One day, somewhere, Allah would provide the sail-maker who understood, for you do not rush these things. You let them mature.

Meantime there was work to be done.

The yard, my research told me, needs to be slightly over twice the beam of the yacht. Taking the hint from a passage in Claud Worth, I decided it should stay permanently aloft, windage or no windage (in fact there is remarkably little windage, surprising though it might seem). To keep the yard quiet it needed lifts from the yardarm to masthead and thence to the deck, a halyard for sending the yard aloft, fore-braces from the yard arms to the bowsprit end and back to the bitts, made continuous, and after braces to the counter and back to the cockpit.

Eyes are spliced in the lifts and braces to make a press fit onto the yard-arms. This obviates the need for cumbersome fittings. The fore-brace, which is continuous, runs through a block spliced on shock-cord under the bitts, the object being to keep this brace under continuous tension. The after-braces run through blocks attached to the outer end of the mainsheet horse and back through the after end of the cockpit coaming onto jam cleats. This enables you to brace up the yard with ease, and more importantly to keep tension on the weather after brace, thus supporting the yard arm against the consider-able drive of the sail.

The yard itself is a hollow spruce spar, formerly the mast of a Sprite sail-ing dinghy, adapted and tapered towards the ends, set somewhat forward of the mast to allow bracing, run up on a jackstay, which *Sauntress* already had, and once sent up can be left there and forgotten until needed. The braces are light 6mm line which, more by luck than judgement, do not interfere with the fore and aft rig.

Worth's remark, "the sail is set flying with three halyards," which was not his method, but an observation of the way the thing was handled on trading ketches, solved the problem of setting the beast, for to keep the yard, with sail attached, on deck, was not a good idea. It was too difficult to send up, too cumbersome, in fact too dangerous, especially in a seaway, to set, as early experiments proved. For to be worthwhile it had to be simple to set and to strike, that elusive ideal, "I have seen the sail got down quite easily by one man in a strong wind."

That left the sail itself. And sure enough, one day in the unlikely setting of a pub in Cornwall, mid-winter, with storms howling, music playing, for it was a jamming session, fiddle, drums, guitar, accordion, not a tourist in sight came the longed for "I would love to try that." Allah, one might say, had provided.

David Buchanan, for that was his name, was the sail-maker. Somewhere in his loft was, as it happens, a great Ratsey and Lapthorn sail, not a square-sail, but of beautiful cloth of unknown vintage, just the right weight as Worth would have agreed, and David, bless him, though he took his time, set to with a will, as between us we set about re-creating something worthy of the boat and his reputation, the first squaresail, I would venture, to be made for a yacht of the size of *Sauntress* for many a year.

Once again *Sauntress* had worked her magic.

The sail measures 16ft on the head, which is twice the beam of the boat, 17 at the foot, which is wider, for I was mindful of leading the weather clew to the stem-head on a reach. The foot is arched, partly for appearance and partly for visibility and the drop is 14ft, again partly for appearance and partly to bring the foot well above the deck, for it is a large sail and has a deep reef.

This last caused some head scratching as the sail was to be sent up on three halyards, for ease of handling and striking, so the reefing system would have to be integral, for you cannot go up on the yard on a vessel the size of *Sauntress*, nor did I wish to lower the yard to reef it.

David's solution, inspired possibly by the buntlines of old, was simple and ingenious. Reefing lines are secured to each earing. They drop down to pulleys stitched on the face of the sail, up to the head again, then down to the next pulley and so on until finally, at the slings passing through an eye in the head and down the back of the sail to the pin rail.

The first time we set this lovely and lovingly made sail, there was a sharp intake of breath. For there, beyond our wildest dreams, was the sail I had seen in my imagination, only the thing was real.

Not only was the dream made reality, but to say the sail pulls like a cart horse would be no exaggeration, and on that most tedious point of sailing, a dead run. But not only on a dead run, for although the yard may be braced no more than 15° or perhaps 20°, bring in the lee clew, pole out the weather clew, ease the weather sheet and it becomes, as William Albert Robinson remarks, something akin to a balloon foresail.

In short, to my delight and surprise, you can carry it on a reach. And not only that, but the main, far from blanketing the sail, as one might suppose, acts in conjunction with the squaresail, feeding it wind on a run or with the wind on the quarter, or, when the squaresail is trying to be a foresail (jib set ahead of it and drawing as well), they palpably work in conjunction, powering the boat up in spectacular fashion.

And no, it does not induce rolling. Remember Claude Worth and his "kept the boat steady." That is precisely what it does. But not only that. The accidental gybe, that fearsome thing of violent crash, sudden heel and threatened broach is in some curious way tamed. Some theoretician will explain the reason. I record it simply as fact.

And should you be on the last breath of a fading following breeze with a mile to go to the mooring?

Set thy squaresail and rejoice.

Grinning from ear to ear.

29

Goodbye to All That

T HE COMPASS ADJUSTER CAME, more used to merchant vessels of
several thousands of tons. Little engineless *Sauntress* fazed him not at
all. "Now south again please," as the skipper laboured with the sweep as we
drifted on the tide in the Colne. "Just one more and I will be finished." And
when he had finished, a magnet here, a magnet there, the deviation card neat-
ly marked up, his modest bill paid, I rowed him ashore.

It is in the best tradition of narratives such as this not to refer to events
ashore, so I will not. Africa however is too far for a summer cruise, so the
reader may draw his own conclusions.

05.06.05 Stone (Pyefleet) to Stone (Walton) crew Judy.

Splendid day, whisked down Wallet by squaresail and double-
reefed main, steadying sail, (meaning the squaresail, this because the centre of effort when running is on the centreline of
the boat) try and fail Deben, drift into the Backwaters on very
young flood, companionable supper at Stone.

Well done Droid and that squaresail!

This was not David's lovely sail, nor the tapered spruce yard, but an ex-
perimental version, old spinnaker pole, recut old spinnaker, turned upside
down with the head cut off, bright red and far from in keeping with *Sauntress*,
but it told us what we needed to know. The thing was viable.

Sauntress had emerged from the yard at Toosey unquestionably a better,
livelier, faster and drier boat (Andrew Balfe, alias Droid, had removed the

116

steel girder down the centre-line amongst many other shipwrighting jobs). The skipper was as free as the proverbial bird and lacked only crew, which was where Judy came in.

For Judy had said she would like to try a sail in a yacht with no engine, which, although I did not know it then was her way of seeing what kind of seaman the skipper might be and whether we were compatible, because if so, she was quite happy to hop on board and sail south with *Sauntress*.

And so it proved.

Final preparations continued. *Sauntress* swung oblivious on the much loved mooring in Pyefleet, The East Coast seduced as ever. The East Coast Old Gaffers Race beckoned, but heart hardened, I slipped the mooring for the very last time.

09.06.05 Pyefleet to Weymouth, crew Judy

Forecast Thames, Dover, Wight variable 3 to 4.

They would call them waypoints now, but to cross the Thames Estuary you need in effect to sail from buoy to buoy, all different distances and different courses, with allowance for tide, depths, and in case you are bedevilled, all the light characteristics noted on the passage planning sheet, thirteen different courses in all.

The variable 3 to 4 should have been warning enough, for it is the Meteorological Office way of saying no wind.

The log takes up the tale:

> 07.00 wind N by E ¼, 1½ hour ebb, Pyefleet, off anchor, main, topsail, jib and foresail.
>
> 08.00 zephyrs, suspicion fog, Colne, dowse squaresail, semi-drift, kedge.
>
> 12.00 SE ½ log 1 mile! Inner Bench Head set big jib. Wind at last.

"I think," said Judy, "we are going backwards." I argued the point feebly, insisting *Sauntress* was moving, which she was, but the tide was moving faster.

So down went the kedge and we waited. An old East Coast racing trick that, slyly lower the kedge out of sight of the opposition and bingo, the opposition disappears astern, open mouthed. Quelling the suspicion that *Sauntress* was trying to tell us she did not want to leave the East Coast, we pressed on

At times the wind filled in a little and we could sail. At others we had barely steerage way, but slowly, painfully slowly, we made the Estuary crossing, to find ourselves, at nightfall, utterly becalmed in the worst possible place, just off the North Foreland, very much in the way of shipping.

"What a night!" reads the log, an entry which rather says it all.

Normally *Sauntress* can be persuaded to keep steerage way when to all appearances there is no wind. Very rare indeed are the times she is completely helpless, but this was one of them. A ship bore down on us, showing red and green the sure sign of a collision course. The flashlight on the main warned her off with not much to spare. We struggled to clear another anchored vessel, set as we were by the tide. A pilot vessel buzzed this way and that, especially designed to keep the nerves on edge, and so it went on. But finally dawn came. We had not been run down and daylight revived the spirits.

10.06.05 07.00 S2 log 43 young flood, Ramsgate

But it was a fickle wind still, "becalmed off Dover, working zephyrs," reads the log and once again, God how I hate this place, at the mercy of all the ferries, hovercraft and hydrofoils which that harbour spews forth. We have a VHF but I left it resolutely off, for the last thing we wanted was some peremptory order and enraged officialdom.

Then "fair wind at last, main, topsail, squaresail." And it was the squaresail, drawing in the faint airs when no other sail would, which took us clear. The new wind filled in, rapidly increased and by Folkestone we were down to double-reefed main, romping away at last.

Now we could begin our watch keeping routine. Judy went below, the wind steadied at force 4 NE, and we began to reel off the miles, 52 at 1330, 75 at 1800, 86.5 at 2100, 117 by 0700 the following morning, with the entry "Judy sails us through the night."

Sauntress has been lucky with her crew, be it Chris, Crispin, Georgie and now Judy. It was difficult to avoid the feeling that they were rather better qualified than the skipper, but much too discreet to make the thing obvious.

And something—for all the engineless sailing, the scares in the Downs, the refusal to use technology (to this day I cannot master a waypoint, nor do I wish to), the dinosaur-like clinging to the old ways, as taught in my youth, paper charts, the patent log, the religious keeping of a deck log, the refusal to have anything to do with marinas, the absence of guard rails, (but we do have life lines and an invariable rule, clip on when on watch at night, in bad weather or reefing), the absence of a life raft—something kept bringing them back.

It must be the boat.

That she is photogenic is beyond doubt. Time and time and time again she appears, often unacknowledged, in magazines, in books, even on television as representing whatever it is that has the cameras clicking.

But she is also able, fast, comfortable, beautifully balanced, strong, blessed with an ability to keep moving when lesser craft wallow, handy as a Una Boat, for she can wriggle through the narrowest channel. In short a delight to sail and a tribute to her designer, Wright, in Cardiff, all those years ago.

11.06.05. *Wind Ne 2/3, all sail including squaresail, run*

We lost the wind again of course, that certain precursor of a wind change and spent the night drifting between St Catherine's Point and The Needles well out to sea, but inside the shipping lanes, so this time nothing to worry about.

"But surely it takes much longer?" I hear you say. Well, yes, obviously it does. But a sailing boat is neither a motor car, nor an aeroplane. You do not go to sea in a sailing yacht in order to meet schedules, for there is no slower means of locomotion on the planet. Even a bicycle is faster. You go to sea for the pleasure of the thing, and the wind in all its moods, including, if you have no engine, the calms.

Back comes the wind, SW this time, kicking up those horrible hollow seas that mean wind over tide. The boathook went over and we returned to retrieve it, man overboard practice, and succeeded on the second attempt, drifting down, hove to, all quiet, leaned over and pick it up. Simple if you know how.

"What about some lunch Judy?"

We hove to and I made her a Salade Nicoise. A Salade Nicoise, a proper one anyway, is not the work of a moment. Boil your eggs, in sea water of course, wash your lettuce, likewise in sea water, skin your tomatoes, peel and chop your onions, peel and crush the garlic, make a proper dressing, olive oil, salt, pepper, mustard, lemon juice, open the tuna, open the anchovies, add, if you have it, ripe avocado (we did), shell the eggs, add black olives and capers; dish up in the cockpit and you will live like kings.

"Off Portland, jogging along sociably."

But heaven knows, Judy and the skipper deserved a break and if the delay lost us the tide, so be it.

And so indeed it was.

The sea turned nasty in the way it only can off Portland Bill, wind against tide or not, *Sauntress* leapt and wriggled over one vicious short sea after another, the tide and maybe the fringes of the race mocked our best efforts. Something gave way below, the port shelf on which reside the seldom used GPS, binoculars, Walker Log box, torches and so on, depositing the lot on the cabin sole. I had forgotten to screw the thing home.

And, says Judy, the skipper ran out of fags.

The log reads, truthfully I think,

> Wind not so much fills in as develops into a nasty channel storm, wind against tide. Elect a night at anchor, hence Weymouth. Tack in around 2000 Log 220.
>
> Big (and well earned) drink and bed.

30

To Falmouth for Orders

OUT WENT THE FISHING LINE.

The Walker log spun merrily, for how else does the log spin, but merrily? For that merrily implies all is well with the world, the boat running before a quartering sea, main sheeted out, Portland Bill receding to a smudge on the horizon, Georgie intent, as ever, on catching us tea, supper, breakfast, a mackerel most likely, to be snatched aboard in wriggling triumph, scales everywhere, gutted and no sooner in the pan. A squeeze of lemon, a hunk of good brown bread, "watch the gybe, Georgie, watch the gybe," for steering the course and fishing are not compatible, but yes, undeniably, a fish or better fishes, caught from your own vessel, taste so much better.

But Portland is not to be so easily dismissed. "If the inside passage is taken, the navigation will require great care, unless the yacht is equipped with an auxiliary engine, for arrival off the Bill of Portland must be timed to coincide with high water Dover. To arrive at the wrong time involves the risk of the yacht being swept into the race, particularly if she is early." So writes Adlard Coles in the delightful *Sailing Days*, published in 1944.

Close tacking out of Weymouth harbour, we had picked up the forecast easterly, force 3 or thereabouts, to time our arrival, precisely as directed, at high water Dover. Soon however it began to fail. Too late to change our minds we were swept, with ever increasing speed, towards the race. "It is said," continues Adlard Coles, "that a yacht cannot strike the Bill as the tide sweeps her away, but I doubt this." And he is right. It is here that Anne Davison and her husband lost *Reliance*, only a few years after those lines were written.

We neither hit the rocks, nor were swept into the race, for a providential breath settled matters and away, once again, we went.

It is seventy miles from Portland to Prawle Point, a passage that Adlard Coles describes as "exacting." But then he, like us, sailed without an auxiliary engine which, if not a rarity at the time he was writing, and he was speaking of the inter-war years, was by no means common.

"Three miles off Salcombe, moon, beam reach," a little land breeze that, to tease and fail again, for by dawn came the entry "log 83.5, George becalmed."

The new wind when it came was NW, a close reach to St Anthony, plenty of wind funnelling out through the narrows, a smart beat up to pick up a mooring off the hallowed portals, and who can resist hallowed portals, of the Royal Cornwall Yacht Club.

In short a classic West Bay passage.

Georgie, for the last time, bid adieu. For thirty years he had crewed *Sauntress*, unfailingly cheerful, unfailingly cool, wildlife-mad, fishing crazy, a trifle accident-prone usually due to his own strength, Georgie was synonymous with *Sauntress*.

It was sad to see him go.

Falmouth, largely due to Georgie, for this was home territory to him, was hospitable to a fault. Such matters as pilot books, Ocean Passages for the World, pretentious or what, but, I am sorry, relevant to the engineless *Sauntress*, sextant checked, were mixed with parties ashore, hospitality, hospitality and more hospitality, lunches which lasted to midnight, strawberries and champagne, membership of those hallowed Portals, in honour, that, of another mentor, should they but know it.

I waited for the weather and Judy. Yes, another convert to Sauntress, Judy.

For now at last new horizons really beckoned

And the mentor?

Think of, say Wilfred Thesiger, or Patrick Leigh Fermor, or Bill Tilman, or Blondie Hasler, and you have the archetypical gentleman loner, ascetic, learned, lean, weather-beaten, half romantic, half practical, utterly fearless, deeply conservative but with a strong anarchic streak, restless, visionary, product of Empire despite themselves; and you have another such, unsung, and his name was Kenneth Whitehead.

And in just the same mould, decorated in the war but never speaking of it, seconded by the War Office to the Royal Iraqi Army just before the regicide, mountaineer, yachtsman, classicist, a bachelor all his days, this was the man who, walking away from shore life, living with the utmost frugality, took his tiny strip-planked Grand Diable French built yacht called *Clairon* to the world of the classical Mediterranean, long before flotilla holidays, mobile phones, GPS or marinas were ever thought of.

And it was my great good fortune to go with him, summer after summer after summer. This is a world you can now only read about in books, perhaps sighing for what is lost. Not for Kenneth the fleshpots of the French Riviera, for he was seeking, as I subsequently sought, the wilder shores, the near forbidden places, the scruffy little towns; if truth be known, dusty and sleepy forgotten backwaters, deserted inlets, the mouldering Venetian settlements in Tito's Yugoslavia, or the blistering heat of the wildest of wild Greek places, the virtually inaccessible Mani peninsula; all these and more were grist to his mill.

For here, with his beloved Admiralty Pilot, his library of such as the *Iliad*, Herodotus, Homer, *Tartarin of Tarascon*, a demijohn of whatever local wine was on offer, his Abdullah cigarette screwed into long holder, his monocle, his erudition and his sense of history, he was at home. For Kenneth was a traveller in the true sense of the word, eating what the locals ate, drinking what the locals drank, flying, to the confusion of the natives, the salt stained ensign of the Royal Ocean Racing club, ships' stamp at the ready, for he understood the bureaucrat's love of such things; *Clairon*, with gold sovereigns in the bilges, explored and explored and explored.

And the sovereigns were there for a purpose. For in these wild parts, gold, the coin the reluctant official or sweating mechanic would test with his teeth, was worth far more than banknotes.

And Kenneth knew it.

The *Bora*, that fearsome wind screaming down the mountains, a monochrome world of white rock, whitecaps and intensely blue sky and sea, its coming heralded—for his eye was sharp—by that little cloud on the mountain top suddenly descending; the *Sirocco*, that enervating southerly wind from the African furnace which had all and sundry tetchy and irritable, and poor *Clairon*'s timbers opening in the heat; the stone cold meals—for no true Greek would eat hot food, dangerous for the health, they said; the slap, slap, slap of the old crone tenderising octopus on the rocks; and occasionally, miraculously, swordfish steak and mezes which made the rest of the meal redundant.

This, for a youth from the grey northern climes was heady stuff indeed, long gone but never to be forgotten.

31

Biscay

B Y A MERCY THE ADMIRALTY HAVE NOT QUITE thrown to the winds the accumulated wisdom of generations of seamen from the age of sail. Only just, mark you, for there is a needlessly apologetic tone to Chapter 8, Admiralty *Ocean Passages for the World*, but the little that has survived is enough.

"Make westing, young man, make westing," says the Admiral in so many words.

And that to us made eminent sense and for several reasons. First, as the Admiral says, "it must be borne in mind that the prevailing winds and currents have a tendency to set towards the Ile d'Ouessant and into the Bay of Biscay when south of it," adding trenchantly, "in no case should Ile d'Ouessant be sighted." In the second place, once in 10° to 12°W, we would be outside all the southbound shipping lanes. And in the third, psychology this, once out there it would be too late for cold feet.

Judy appeared armed with white collision flares and the aptly named Biscay Cake, all sticky fruit for nibbling on long night watches. We telephoned, as you can for a modest fee, our very own meteorological expert, who promised stable NW to NE becoming E winds over the ensuing five days. I played with traverse tables, passage planning, lights, nominal ranges, distances, tidal set, leeway, pretty much until heart's content and with, as both later admitted, a stomach more queasy than a final goodbye dinner entirely justified, took, as they say, our departure.

PJ and Verity, our hosts in Falmouth, waved us goodbye, and for the hell of it we set that blood red squaresail, streamed the log and were gone.

08.07.05. Crew Judy.

Time 1100. wind direction/force NNW2. Visibility good. Course 170°. Log streamed. Tidal set/leeway ebb. DR/Fix Pendennis. Other. Goodbyes.

The old routine again.

The wind played momentary tricks off the Lizard and then settled into the promised NNW 2/3, with nothing to report. The Walker log tells you all you need to know about your speed through the water, a kind of obsession that, as you watch the little dial, how many miles can we sail this watch? No cheating now. None of that stupid flickering dancing and irritating GPS business, just the world's simplest piece of clockwork, mark an estimated position on the chart, steer the course and enjoy the simplicity of it all. A momentary check on the GPS gives us a fix. We correct the course a little and sail on. By 1100 on the following day we have run 103 nautical miles, Ushant is satisfactorily invisible. The wind has veered to N by E 2/3 and, this being a longish passage, we bother little with log entries, just enough to keep an eye on things.

"Biscay quiescent, strange popples, breakers, up-wellings" tell us what? That we are off the continental shelf, that sudden plunge from hundreds to several thousand metres (should be fathoms really), which in bad weather would be wicked.

Night falls.

And, I am delighted to say, it is my watch.

No moon.

The odd trawler about, but the stars, my goodness the stars. Out, I suppose, should come the clichés. The no chance for second thoughts is obviously right. Here we are at least 100 miles from any port, under a night sky to die for, a caressing breeze, all sail set, Judy below, so find a star, position it in the rigging, under the cross-trees will do nicely, and keep it there. In an hour or so find another, for the heavens are wheeling, and repeat. Towards the end of your watch, find the small torch, read the patent log, mark up the chart, wake Judy and hand over.

10.07.05. 1100. E by N 4. Visibility good. Log 205. 215° Compass.
GPS 47.32 N 07.17W, days' run 98.5.

Morning of 10th set all and hope for a good run today.

[Wait for it.]

Dolphins.

The icing on an already glittering cake. With all set, *Sauntress* racing south by
west to clear Finisterre, they come tumbling from afar. Judy is on the helm
so now I can lie on the foredeck and watch as they gambol under the bow. It
is not our fault that this is proving such a perfect passage, the yacht is loving
it, we are loving it, Biscay is showing an absurdly benign face, the horrors of
the Downs, Dover and Portland do not even cross our mind. The square sail
is doing its stuff. The boat is easy on the helm. There is no shipping. Just that
easy loping routine.

Day melts into night and back into day again.

1100 E 4 (the wind is veering all the while). Course 210. Log 323.
123 nautical miles in 24 hours. Best run?

Yes, I believe so. BBC long-wave is still in range. The evening forecast comes:
"Fitzroy E 5-7."

More wind. Reef and dowse jib. 100 miles to go.

Blue turns to grey. There is not exactly spite in the wind, but it has piped
up a fair bit. We elect for Coruña, nip across the shipping lanes, a remarkable
procession, first northbound, then southbound, or maybe vice versa, better
crossed in the last of the light, and settle down to a rough old sail, nothing
Sauntress cannot handle, but on a course now to raise the Galician coast upwind of Coruña for all the reasons one does such a thing. With the wind veering and strengthening we want room to run off, not a nasty beat at the end of
the passage.

Sauntress has just the sail she needs. Two reefs in the main, jib furled (I run off to shadow the sail whilst doing that, no unnecessary flogging), lifelines are attached, the boat is now nursed a little, luffing slightly to the harder gusts, but racing still through the night, a wild but in no way anxious ride.

> Judy reports wave filled the cockpit last night—I report maybe force 7—but *Sauntress* very comfortable—barograph tumbling now (note, barograph, not barometer, so you can see from the trace just what the pressure is doing), fog, then sun also very close encounter with ship in fog.
> 1107 E by N 5 plus. Visibility moderate. Course 210. Log 440.
> Off Galicia. Day's run 117. [Obsessed, as ever, by the day's run].

"You had better shake out the reef or set the square sail," remarked Judy as we tidied ourselves and the ship up for landfall. I set the faithful square sail once more. We rounded the breakwater, handed the log, picked up a buoy, furled the sails and went to explore this new and interesting place.

Four days and four hours. 452 nautical miles. Casualty one lamp chimney. And Judy's verdict?

"I have never felt safer on a ship."

32

A Day at the Races

"TIS A MOORING YOU WILL BE WANTING" said Jose, Galicia being Ireland and vice versa, and as promptly laid one. But what about Africa a little voice says? Africa can wait, you reply for we had stumbled, *Sauntress* and her skipper, on old fashioned manners admirably suited to an old fashioned boat, and here for a while we could stay.

There emerged, from where I could not say, a mercurial figure called Tojo. Those familiar with the works of William Albert Robinson will recognise the type, for he embarked for his world cruise one Etera. Etera, alias Tojo, was fearless, diminutive, had an extraordinary knack of attracting the girls, was totally unworldly, had to be rescued from sundry escapades and was completely irresistible.

Sauntress once again had a crew.

But first there was Galicia to be explored.

We lay at anchor in an almost landlocked bay, in blistering heat, perspiration dripping, like a couple of beached whales, waiting, in a sense, for something to happen. We had been roped into a regatta, a local affair of traditional boats, had explored all the bars the village had to offer, whilst Tojo, in his inimitable way, had the measure of all in the village. And the village pleased him.

The afternoon wore on, ever hotter, ever more still, gay bunting, little children playing on the beach, the perfect picture of a minor paradise when, of a sudden, Tojo pointed with wonderment, up the bay.

Where, it appeared, a thousand devils were whipping the tranquil waters to a fury. No sooner had the word Williwaw formed on the skipper's lips than we leapt into action. Oars removed from the inflatable, second anchor down we waited for the thing to strike. *Sauntress* heeled violently, the inflatable took to the air before clamping itself on the cockpit, the anchors snubbed, held a moment and then dragged and before we knew it we were down amongst the moorings, careering shoreward until something caught, *Sauntress* brought up and we could survey the devastation.

The bunting was in tatters. Boats fled in all directions. Happy little voices had turned to screams of fear and disbelief.

And as soon as it had come, it was gone again.

Welcome to Galicia.

And that little blast blew us into the arms of Redes, home for several years now to *Sauntress*, the skipper and Etera, alias Tojo.

Not long after that episode and the laying of the mooring appeared a neat bearded figure by the name of Paco. We had seen his boat soon enough, a gaff cutter like ours, as neat as her owner, trim and short-ended, bluff bowed, boxy cabin, transom stern, in a sense the antithesis of *Sauntress* and, had we but known it, long the ruler of this particular roost.

And this Paco, with an invader on his patch, metaphorically pawed the ground, flared the nostrils and issued a challenge.

Honour demanded we accept.

Local boy against interloper, sinewy grace against boxy competence, there was a momentary stir of interest in the little village that is Redes, bets were surreptitiously placed, sides taken; "cutlasses between teeth," smiled Paco wickedly who promptly trounced a bewildered *Sauntress* in the first of five.

The groan was almost audible. The outsider is all bluster. The king was not about to be toppled from the castle. The second race was closer, much closer, but by now we were left with a mountain to climb.

"Your mainsail is baggy. Your topsail backs," announced Paco smugly. That was silly of him.

Stung, we set to work.

It is called tuning the boat. Rather, I suppose, as people tune motor cars, to release the potential. There are such things as mast rake, luff tension, correct lead of sheets, proper ballasting, all these and more make the difference between win and lose in a five-hour race, and especially to windward. And it was to windward that the graceful *Sauntress* was being trounced and it hurt.

But wounded pride does wonders.

Two more races and we were even.

Now the village had something to bet on. Now interest quickened. Two camps developed, rather to our surprise, for outsiders or no, we had our backers, "tie a bucket on his keel," "go out and win," take him down a peg or two, I think I hear you say.

And blow me, we did.

Now blood was well and truly up. Stung to the quick Paco hit back. An event was tacked onto the Redes regatta, the "Desafio Redes/Irlanda." The first was a washout, no wind, the next he won, preening like the proverbial turkey cock. *Sauntress* hit back in turn. And hit back again, and again. And dammit, again.

And silly, or childish, though all this may sound, it has done wonders for both boats. For added to her other abilities is an ability now to out-sail just about anything on the water. Running backstays have helped, judicious ballasting too, a new main some more, taut luffs still more and so every July for several years two old men joust on the water, others join in, the event grows.

33

La Costa de la Muerte

"THIS COAST," says the Spanish *Admiralty Pilot*, "requires great caution in order to avoid the numerous reefs and isolated dangers, some of them at a considerable distance from the coast, the navigator having always to bear in mind the (uncertain) currents."

The British *Admiralty Pilot* is scarcely more encouraging, but then again he seldom is, dwelling at length on the perils to be expected, magnetic anomalies, fog, lights obscured by cloud, the absence of ports of refuge, the danger of closing the land in bad visibility and sundry other admonitions.

We were getting soft, a little too comfortable. Tojo was fidgeting, *Sauntress* too, so it was time for a bit of adventure.

Corme, about 40 miles westwards, is a small port on the Costa de La Muerte. East from here we had already been, mildly challenging, especially Cedeira with its tricky leading line entrance under high cliffs, rebounding waves and fickle winds, but crew was becoming mutinous.

We got our adventure.

A drift in the morning, waiting for the wind, was to be expected. The wind came sure enough, north-east and whisked us, on a dead run, past the point of no return, namely Coruña, and then filled in as fast as we could reef. Down came the topsail. In went the first reef and then the second. For a while it was enough.

Then the Islas Sisargas came and the wind wound up another notch. A glorious day, blue sky, sparkling but ever more boisterous seas, we surfed and plunged faster and ever faster.

We roared down a wave and buried the bow.

Impressive and dangerous. In fact it had never happened before.

I went below and secured the fore-hatch.

Up into what was to all intents and purposes a sudden gale we scrambled in the last reef. Tojo, in a gesture of glorious insouciance started to fish.

Sauntress was still going far too fast, but with a few miles only to go we hung on. The danger obviously was a broach. Breakers showed whitely ahead and we dodged an unexpected reef.

A fishing boat, rolling and plunging, appeared. Shamelessly I followed it. Round the point expecting shelter the wind came whistling in squalls off the land. Corme was now upwind, so upwind we must go.

And in the proverbial welter of foam we shot into the harbour, short tacked up the head and anchored.

The effect ashore was electric.

If the natives had crawled over *Sauntress* "the wooden boat" in Coruña, Corme the wild west of the Costa de la Muerte would not leave her alone. Tojo, of course, understood the language, deep Galego here. The greybeards had watched and not seen anything like it for years.

In short we were fêted.

It was a remarkable passage and a remarkable experience. Day after day the north-easter howled. Boat after boat came in, sails damaged, crew exhausted, anchors dragging. We struck the square yard, laid out a second anchor and basked not only in the uniquely Galician hospitality of the place, but the glorious wildness, the crystal clear waters, the contraband everything and of course that sense of achievement such a passage brings.

"Cape Verde Islands?" muttered Tojo yet again.

And why not, I say.

34

Shadows Chasing on a Hillside

T HE NORTH-EASTER BLEW AND BLEW. Our plans to go south lay in tatters for time was running out. I amused myself with the chart and the shadows of the clouds, something akin to Sherlock Holmes and those telegraph poles from a railway carriage window.

If it takes X for a shadow to travel Y, then it must be travelling at a certain speed. The upshot of this idle speculation was force 8 and well I could believe it. The square yard struck, the boom secured smack fashion on the transom, fisherman and bower anchor down, all held. Others were less lucky, and much shouting and roaring of mighty motors was the upshot as yacht after yacht got into difficulties.

But *Sauntress*, with nearly 100 years under her keel, was not of their world. Our mentors come from a different age. O'Brien, Commander Graham and Claud Worth, especially Claud Worth. And when their names appear in these pages, it is not out of some desire to place our modest adventures on the same pinnacles as these, heaven forfend.

But they speak to me. And, in a way, they speak to *Sauntress* too.

> "Custom can never lessen the wonder of a boat. First the conception in the brain of the designer. Then the long months of creation while, by the labour of many men, wood and metal are slowly wrought into the form and semblance of a boat, but as yet a mere inert mass of material. Then the supreme moment of her launch—her birth—when, taking life from wind and sea, she seems a sentient living thing, responsive and obedient to sym-

pathetic management, but stubborn and perverse with those who do not understand her moods."

—Claud Worth. *Yacht Cruising.*

"*Sauntress* punished her skipper for this unseamanlike behaviour by crashing up and down and going nowhere. Shamed, the topsail was reset, having been struck in the previous squall, and she bore away happily as we tacked slowly up the coast."

—The author. Log of a cruise to Brest.

This sentient being, as Claud Worth puts it, has, I think, to be built of wood. Talk to any shipwright, I mean a proper shipwright and he will agree. The designer, the craftsman and the skipper, without all three *Sauntress* could not be *Sauntress*. And yes, she has her moods, although those moods are in fact telling the skipper he is doing something wrong, pinching her unduly, too much sail, not enough sail, ballasting wrong, sheet leads wrong, but get it right and my goodness does she reward you.

And perhaps after 40-odd years more is right than is wrong, the ear-to-ear-grin of a guest on the helm tells you that, the boat full of life, vigour and strength.

But there is something else. The gaff rig, to the casual observer, is picturesque, archaic even, all those lines, mainsail, topsail, foresail, jib and in our case squaresail too. A lot of work. Well, yes it is if you want to get the best of your yacht, but it is also forgiving.

Here is Worth again:

"In the case of the ordinary rigs [he means gaff rig] which have been tried by long experience, short of the loss of the mast there is no accident which cannot be repaired at sea or for which an efficient jury rig cannot be improvised with sufficient sea room."

Note the sea room.

Off Ares, in our Ria, known locally as the ventilator for the squalls it pro-
duces, we had set out for a little sail, all set including topsail. The Ria is four
miles wide, but never will I sail on the lee shore, for you never know. I hug the
weather shore as a matter of principle.

"Throat halyard breaks off Ares. Strike topsail, rig jury and return to
mooring," the living proof of Claud Worth's assertion. The accident was a
small one, in sheltered waters, but we had sea room, time to think the problem through, and a spare halyard to the masthead with which to rig an improvised throat halyard.

> "Having on several occasions been hove to in bad weather,
> sometimes from necessity, but far more often in order to take a
> spell during a heavy turn to windward, I consider the ability to
> lie to safely under short canvass to be of supreme importance in
> a sea going yacht."
>
> —Claud Worth, *Yacht Cruising.*

Now look back over these pages and see just how often *Sauntress* has hove to.
The point I am making here is that these are not just bed-side books. They
are for us, sailing a yacht contemporary in rig and build, a supremely useful
source of advice, comfort and, at times amusement.

Ares is the next village to Redes.

> "We carry a ton of water in four tanks [this is *Tern III* displacing
> 28 tons TM] but we had not economised at all, and did not care to
> take water from a water boat. So we sailed to Ares Bay, a beautiful
> little cove in the head of Coruña Bay, where according to the Sail-
> ing Directions, there is a spring close to the beach. Armour and
> Alf went ashore with the canvass water breakers. They found the
> spring, of excellent water [they all are here, I can vouch for that],
> but it was more than a mile from the beach. Fortunately they met
> Mr Shallis, an English resident, who very kindly hired an ox cart

for us the next morning. The ox proved to be a diminutive but industrious cow, who had already been led round the village for the
direct supply of milk to the inhabitants."

—Claud Worth. *West by South. Tern III* 1920.

And Mr Shallis? Well, Ferrol is just over the way, the great Naval Dockyard, a clinker dinghy, such as one I have just built, is
known as a "bote ingles," such names as Vickers Armstrong
crop up in local history now and again. Not all Spanish Armada. And help with the dinghy? Yes, even that, for no oak crooks
could I find, but "for knees and breasthook apple crooks are
best of all, both for toughness and appearance."—Claud Worth.
Yacht Cruising.

And in a garden somewhere, yes, there was a fallen apple tree. And he is right
about the appearance, that lovely swirling grain.

But in other respects things are different. Sails are no longer made of
Egyptian cotton or canvas or halyards from hemp. (But decks are nonetheless
payed with pitch, we carry red lead, white lead, leather, neat's-foot oil, waxed
twine, no less than three anchors and oil lamps). Nor do we wind the chronometer. For we have no need. The GPS is there for that, though the sextant
too, against the day, and we have wireless.

Worth in 1920 did not, or not as we would understand it.

"Ferrol is one of the principal naval dockyards of Spain and of
course has a wireless installation, so next morning we took one
of our timekeepers ashore and called at the Admiral's office to
ask permission to visit the chronometer house. The officer in
command was most kind and anxious to help, but it turned out
the dockyard possessed one chronometer, which had been allowed to run down.

He said, however, that if we cared to wait until tomorrow…
we might care to listen to the Paris time signal ourselves."

He passes no comment, so nor shall I.

We are near the end. I have tried, in these pages, to show what it is like to sail the way our forebears did. I am blessed by owning an exceptional boat. It took time to summon up the courage to remove the engine, but once done I have never once regretted it. We have tried, in our modest way, to be adventurous, to sail as far as time permitted and usually to what I have chosen to call wilder shores.

For here you will find old fashioned courtesy, an understanding of the ways of the sea, as well as romance and an escape from the insanity of the modern world.

In short I have lived my dream and for that I have no regrets. And one day, maybe, if Tojo says it often enough, *Sauntress* will spread her wings once more, and propelled by that squaresail, go in search of even wilder shores.

But we have not finished yet, or at least not quite yet, for the last word belongs to none other than our old friend and mentor, that glorious half-forgotten thoroughly Victorian figure,

Claud Worth.

35

Pons Asinorum

"TIME AND RIGHT ASCENSION," wrote Claud Worth, "are the *pons asinorum* of navigation" adding, as you reel rather before such erudition,

"The subject is not really difficult."

Well of course it is. It ties the brain in knots. You scrabble to remember, if you ever knew, sines, cosines, versines, azimuth, Greenwich hour angle, zenith distance, dip, parallax, ecliptic, polar distance, the PZX triangle, index error…

Yet some of us still try.

Why?

The answer, surprising though it may seem, is that I feel safer. Brought up to find my way around by Walker trailing log, compass course, tidal triangles, dead reckoning, allowance for leeway, buoy hopping, passage planning, paper chart, deck log, call it what you will, these are old familiar friends which cannot fail.

True we now have a hand held GPS, switched on once a day as a check on the EP, but true too that down below are the sextant, the almanac, the tables, the wireless for the time signal and the shipping forecast.

Or as Don Street, he of the engine-less *Iolaire* puts it, the most essential piece of navigational equipment in the world is eye-ball mark one, given to all of us by God at birth.

And that, with lead line, is actually all you need.

Amazing innit?

For as with the absence of an engine, you are suddenly freed from the expense, the irritation, the breakdowns, the frustration, the need for marinas, for you are no longer a slave to dials, screens, buttons or all the paraphernalia that has come to be regarded as essential.

Free to get on with the business in hand, which is sailing your craft, in reasonable safety, from A to B, an eye on the weather, an eye on the sails, an eye on the pennant at the masthead, a reef or two for the gusts, life line attached, doing what you are supposed to do when you go to sea in a yacht.

Which is to enjoy yourself.